0129823   AUSDEN, K.   Up the
crossing
B/AUS   AS 8/81   6.50

-7 OCT. 1985

Please renew/return this item by the last date shown.

So that your telephone call is charged at local rate,
please call the numbers as set out below:

	From Area codes 01923 or 0208:	From the rest of Herts:
Renewals:	01923 471373	01438 737373
Enquiries:	01923 471333	01438 737333
Minicom:	01923 471599	01438 737599

L32b

7 AUG 1995

15 APR 1996   **3 1 AUG 2004**   1/7/08

16 JUN 2007 Derbyshire

- 3 MAY 1996

12/10/11

1 3 SEP 2001

6/12

2 5 JUN 2008

L 33

L32/rev79

D0832531

UP THE CROSSING

Ken Ausden

UP THE CROSSING

Illustrated by
Phillida Gili

British Broadcasting Corporation

Published by the
British Broadcasting Corporation
35 Marylebone High Street
London W1M 4AA

First published 1981

ISBN 0 563 17902 3

Printed in England

by Spottiswoode Ballantyne Ltd., Colchester, Essex

The BBC *Woman's Hour* serial based on this book was produced by
Pat McLoughlin. It was adapted by Janet Hickson and read by
Geoffrey Matthews

Contents

Foreword

Without doubt, the town of Swindon was created by the Great Western Railway.

Old Swindon, a small market town on a hilltop two miles away, had been in existence for a good many centuries before Brunel chose his spot to build a railway factory on the main line between London and Bristol.

But the new model township, which Isambard Kingdom Brunel planned and M. Digby Wyatt designed, grew up during the 1840s. It consisted of some five hundred workers' cottages plus facilities unheard of at the time – a school, a church, a Mechanics' Institute and a Medical Fund Society. The recent restoration of the original 'railway village' has ensured Swindon's place in the history of industrial Britain as a fine example of a town created and built by a railway company.

Swindon expanded over the next one hundred years but, like many another industrial town, its popularity never matched its growth rate. Despite its proximity to the incomparable Wiltshire downs, precious few people who didn't live there loved the Swindon of the 1930s.

They may have recognised it as a place where they built railway engines – unarguably the best! – or with a junction station where one occasionally changed trains.

But positively not a place to love - or live in – or even visit!

But we lived there – and we loved it. And many of us still do. It may not be the railway town it once was, in its heyday employing fifteen thousand men, but those of us who grew up in the glorious age of steam were surely privileged beyond measure. (How can one not feel sorry for the successive generations of boys who have been 'up the crossing' or 'down Hay Lane' to watch the present-day trains go by? Who could possibly fall in love with a diesel electric?)

The thirties was a unique and fascinating decade, happier perhaps for the children than for their parents. Fear of unemployment and approaching war touched us only fleetingly. This book is about the late thirties. It all happened in a railway town – but the book is not all about railways.

It is not truly autobiography. Whilst every chapter has its feet firmly planted in truth, its head is sometimes hidden in clouds of fantasy.

Many of the people and places certainly existed, but for various reasons names may have changed and occasional characters and situations are pure invention.

This book is for all those who grew up in the thirties, the halcyon years 'before the war' – and especially those with steam in their veins.

And, of course, for those who would have liked to have been there with us!

Trip Day

In 1938 I was twelve.

All the kids down our street were twelve. Or there-abouts. Vic might have been thirteen: Georgie may have been only ten or eleven. But we averaged out at around twelve.

Perhaps being born in the year of the General Strike made us a bit special. Growing up with the means test, appeasement, abdication, rearmament and such-like barely understood words must have had some effect.

The thirties meant many things to many people. All roads led to September 1939. But first there was 1938. I don't exactly remember whether it was an exceptionally good summer or a particularly bad winter. And yet I have vivid recollections of individual days and the way in which we lavished ourselves on them.

I remember especially the summer of 1938. By summer, I mean the day we went to the seaside. Trip Day.

We always broke up for the summer holidays the first Friday in July. Nowhere else in England did they start their holiday as early as we did. At least, not as far as I could ever find out. But we had to fall in line with the railway factory, seeing that about three-quarters of the kids' fathers worked for the GWR. And the factory always closed the first complete week in July.

Another funny thing, too – and I certainly never heard of this happening anywhere else – we finished school Friday dinner-time. There was no such thing as school dinners in those days. Two minutes after the head monitor had rung the heavy brass bell in the entrance hall at twelve o'clock on the last day of term, the place was deserted.

As soon as I'd had my dinner – we always had meat roll and mash Fridays – I'd call for my mates Albie and Vic and we'd be off down the sidings at twenty to the dozen. It was a train spotter's heaven. Little tank engines were shunting coaches everywhere. Giant locos were getting up steam ready for the great exodus. It was glorious, organised chaos.

The first trip trains, carrying the lucky families who could afford a whole week's holiday, would be setting off for Penzance and Tenby and Aberystwyth in the evening. All the long haul stuff would be shifted before midnight. The trains for the day-trippers – to Weston and Weymouth and Barry Island – would be ready that night for an early start in the morning. Families tended to go to the same place every year. Georgie's lot had been going to Weston for the Day Trip Saturday ever since Brunel's railway works had been built. Vic got dragged off to London, which seemed daft to the rest of us kids – including Vic – as there's a well-known shortage of sand and sea and piers in London, but Vic's Dad said there was more to do if it rained.

Our family always went to Weymouth. Ever since I could remember. We were just a nice compartment full, our mob. My Mum and Dad, my younger brother and baby sister, our Gran, Uncle Tom and Auntie Ethel, and old Mr Pinnock who lived in the end house all by himself and everybody felt sorry for.

There were three trains for Weymouth. The railway works took over the beach for the day. We must have pretty near outnumbered the local population.

The trains departed from the sidings at seven-forty, eight-ten and nine o'clock. We always had tickets for the seven-forty. Well, I mean, you might as well make a full day of it when you only get one day a year by the sea.

The pandemonium in our house started around five o'clock. I was always glad to hear the first stirrings because, apart from Christmas Eve, it was the longest night of the year. Me and our kid never shut our eyes all night.

'Come on you kids,' our Mum would call as she slip-slopped her way downstairs in her furry slippers with bobbles on. 'I want you two washed an' out o' that scullery afore your Gran gets up.'

We didn't need telling twice.

'Your clean shirts are on the chair-back – I've whitened your daps an' they're out dryin' on the coal-bunk – wash your necks proper an' don't splash water all over my clean floor!'

Then Dad came down, yawning and scratching and not looking at all holidayish. He sharpened his cut-throat razor on the smooth leather strap that hung on the back door.

'Who's 'ad me kettle?' he demanded.

'I've made a pot o' tea,' my mother said.

'That was me shavin' water!'

'You know very well Gran 'as to 'ave 'er cup o' tea afore she can get 'er legs goin'.'

'Where's me teeth?' asked Gran.

She started every day off with the same question. She knew jolly well where her teeth were – in the coronation mug on the draining board – but she had to let us all know she was up and ready to be waited on.

[11]

'Will you get these kids out o' this scullery,' my Father yelled. 'If one o' them joggles me arm again I'll cut me flamin' throat an' then there won't be no Trip Day for nobody!'

'Come an' 'ave your cornflakes, you two. You're goin' nowhere on an empty stomach,' said my mother. 'An' Gran – will you stop polishin' them teeth an' get 'em i your 'ead!'

Dead on seven, Uncle Tom and Auntie Ethel arrived. I liked my Uncle Tom. He'd been in the navy in the war. He told me hair-raising stories about what went on in the boiler-room on H.M.S. *Hood* – apart from stoking the boilers.

He always looked smart on Trip Day, did Uncle Tom. The collar of his best cream cricket shirt was neatly turned over the collar of his blue blazer with the gold anchor embroidered on the pocket. His light grey flannel trousers were sharply creased, and he wore a smashing pair of black, patent leather shoes with little bits of snakeskin let in the sides.

I never noticed what Auntie Ethel wore. Not liking her, I suppose I never really looked at her.

'Come on, Gran. Put your shoes on.'

'Which ones shall I wear?'

'Wear your black 'uns with the buckles.'

'They makes me feet sweat!'

'Well, wear your best pair.'

'They got heels. I can't wear heels on that soft sand. We should've gone to Dawlish like I been sayin' for years. Why can't I wear these shoes I got on?'

'Wear your wellies, if you like, Gran, but for goodness' sake 'urry up.'

I went and knocked up old Mr Pinnock. He must have been waiting with his hand on the latch judging by the speed with which he opened the door.

[12]

'Mornin', young feller-me-lad. All set for the off, are we?'

'Gonna be a nice day, Mr Pinnock.'

'Sun's up too soon. It'll rain afore noon.'

Old Pinnock had a dismal rhyme for every occasion!

We trooped along Station Road in a straggling line, occasionally getting tangled up with other family groups. Me and Uncle Tom led the way with my kid brother trotting at our heels trying to keep up with us. Then came Auntie Ethel and my Dad loaded down with enough food to last a regiment a fortnight, and a bit behind them my Mum and the pushchair. The push-chair was piled high with towels, bathing costumes, cricket bat, buckets and spades and enough spare cloth-ing for the regiment to cope with blizzards, floods and other vagaries of the British summer. Underneath this lot, if you looked carefully, you might find my baby sister.

Trailing along some twenty yards in the rear – and falling steadily further behind every minute – were Gran and Mr Pinnock.

'Come on, Gran.'

'Hurry up, Gran.'

'It'll be time to come 'ome afore we gets there if you don't get a move on.'

But Gran, who had just two speeds – dead slow and stop – plodded unhurrying on with an occasional – 'It's all right for you lot. I'm not so young as I was.'

The trip trains did not start from the station platform like ordinary trains. They were all lined up in the sidings outside the railway factory and you walked along the tracks to get to them. I reckon it was the most exciting bit of the whole day, climbing up the special steps to get into the coach.

And then – dead on seven-forty (there was nothing in

the world better to set your watch by than the departure of a GWR train) – the long blast of the guard's whistle, answered promptly by a throaty shriek from the locomotive, like a bird answering its mate.

'What we got to eat, Mum?' says our kid every year regular before the wheels have completed their first revolution.

'Me feet's killin' me. Why didn't you let me wear me best 'uns?' Gran groans.

''Ope you've changed your socks for Trip,' laughs Uncle Tom as Gran kicks off her shoes.

Same routine every year. And I never got tired of it. I wish it could have gone on for ever. I still miss Trip Day.

We just filled a compartment nicely, our lot. And the amount of gear that went up on the luggage rack – you'd have thought we were emigrating!

'Can we go in the corridor, Dad?'

'So long as you stay in sight an' don't go near the door.'

Me and our kid disappear into the corridor with our engine-name-books and pencils and that's the last contact we have with the rest of the family until we're about five minutes from Weymouth. Apart from food supplies being passed out to us about every ten minutes – an apple, a handful of cherries, a slice of lardy cake, a chocolate biscuit, a cream horn . . .

'Give us a 'and with the push-chair,' says Dad as we feel the brakes being applied for the final run in. 'An' 'elp Gran find 'er shoes.'

'Where's the little 'un's rattle got to?' says Mum. 'An' what 'appened to that bag of 'ome-made cakes?'

'A Marks an' Spencer's bag?' asks Gran.

'Yes.'

'It was on the sideboard when I seen it last.'

'Prob'ly still there,' laughs Uncle Tom.

'Nobody'd think of nothin' if it wasn't for me,' grumbles Mum.

But no one is listening. We're all out on the platform watching Dad go through his pockets to find our free passes to show the ticket collector.

From the station to the sea-front is only a few minutes but it seems like hours, what with all the crowd jostling and pushing, and Gran hardly able to walk because her feet have swollen, and one of the push-chair's wheels threatening to fall off any second but – at last – at long, glorious last – there it is! The sea. The sand. The pier. The harbour – and one of the Jersey boats making smoke! The Italian ice-cream parlour. The Punch and Judy show.

All still there – exactly as we left it a year ago.

'Can we 'ave a stick o' rock?' asks our kid.

'Wock! Wock!' yells our baby sister.

'Stop puttin' ideas into 'er 'ead,' my mother chides. 'An' wait till we find ourselves a place on the beach.'

Everywhere people jockeying for the best place so you don't have to pack up and move when the tide comes in – scrabbling for deck-chairs – spreading out towels – staking claim to a few square yards of sand for the next eight hours or so.

By the time Gran and Mr P. have been lowered into their deck-chairs where they take root for the rest of the day, and Dad has got over cussing and sucking his finger which he pinches in a deck-chair every year the same, and Mum has unpacked the push-chair, and Auntie Ethel has had her usual moan about it being too hot or too chilly or too breezy – Uncle Tom and our kid and me are half-way to the sea, Uncle Tom with his grey flannels rolled immaculately to just below his knees, and us two in our itchy, moth-nibbled bathing

[15]

costumes that haven't seen the light of day for twelve months.

'You 'aven't washed your feet, our kid!'

'I never 'ad time. Don't tell our Mum, will you? I'll buy you – a ha'penny cornet if you don't split.'

'Get on in,' shouts Uncle Tom. 'There's enough water there to wash all the engine drivers' feet on the Great Western!'

About an hour later we return to base camp – shivering and covered in goose pimples and swearing we'd loved every minute of it.

'Kept your Gran an' me waitin', you 'ave,' grumbles Mr P. 'Me belly's fair rumblin'.'

''Ave a fish-paste sandwich, Mr Pinnock,' says Mum, on her knees, laying out the feast on the big, stripy bath towels.

'What sort?' demands Mr P. suspiciously.

'Salmon and shrimp.'

'Fishy paste – rotten taste! Got any cheese?'

'Cheese an' tomato.'

'You ain't gone an' put tomato in 'em again,' moans Gran. 'You know them pips gets under me plate!'

'There's some chicken an' 'am rolls if you like. Or blackcurrant jam? Or chocolate spread?'

'Mum, I wanna drink!'

''Ang on a tick. Your Dad's goin' to fetch a tray.'

Dad and Uncle Tom return with a tin tray loaded with white china and a couple of bottles of fizzy lemonade.

''Struth,' says Gran as Dad hands her a cup of tea. ''Ardly 'ad the strength to creep out o' the pot, did it!'

'You'd grumble to be 'ung,' says Dad.

'Should've gone to Dawlish, like I said. Always 'ad a good cup o' tea down there in the old days, me an' Fred did.'

'You can go there nex' year,' Dad threatens, near the end of his tether. 'On your own!'

By this time, our little 'un is yowling her head off just because me and our kid have buried her up to her neck in sand.

'Gerroff, you great bullies,' shouts Mum, clawing away the sand and shaking her clean.

So off we go, me and our kid, up to the ice-cream place where he buys me the promised ha'penny cornet – pink with soft, buttercup yellow ice-cream. And then, without a word, we part – he to the harbour and the boat trains and the ships – and me?

None of them ever knew where I spent the afternoon. It was one of those great secrets that I never shared with anyone. They wouldn't have understood. So I never gave them the chance.

As soon as our kid was out of sight, I was up on the prom and legging it as fast as I could go up towards the big clock. Ten to two! I was going to make it dead on.

Down the steps, two pennies warm in my palm, and up to the ticket office. 'One child, please, mister.'

'Fourpence.'

'I only got tuppence.'

'That's 'ard luck then, ain't it, sonny.'

'Please! I'll sit in the back row. Please!'

''Aven't I seen you before?'

'Yes. A year ago today. You let me in for tuppence then!'

'Did I now?' At last his face cracks. He grins at me. 'All right, then, seein' as 'ow you're a reg'lar! But mind you sits in the back row an' no messin' about!'

Me! Mess about! While the Vaudesques were performing! I don't think the bloke in the ticket office realised that I was about to achieve one of my two real, live shows of the year – the seaside concert party and the

[17]

Christmas pantomime. From the age of eight until the war came and put the mockers on seaside concert parties and turned our local theatre into a cinema, I was totally stage struck. I lived from July to December going through all the routines I picked up from the Vaudesques and from Boxing Day to Trip Day on memories of Cinderella or Robinson Crusoe. I spent countless hours in the shed down the end of our garden writing scripts, sketches, lyrics, and rehearsing one-man spectaculars – tap-dancing, juggling, crooning, comic patter. And nobody ever knew – nobody ever saw me perform. Because I was really a total introvert – I'd have dropped dead from shock if I'd ever had to perform in public.

So there I was, in the back row, the sun lighting the open-air stage, like a pilgrim having reached Mecca, waiting breathlessly for Val Vaux, the comedian, to get the show under way.

'I say, I say, I say – d'you know how to make a Maltese cross with only two matches?'

I hugged myself with joy as the stooge made the traditional response.

'No – how do you make a Maltese cross with two matches?'

Now for it! I could hardly wait for the punch-line.

'Light 'em and stick 'em up 'is jumper!'

I fell about laughing. Nothing had changed. Not even the jokes! One or two new sketches, a fresh blonde soprano (but she was the least important part of the programme – a sort of commercial break for eating sweets and things while she got her cackling over).

When the show had been under way about fifteen minutes, the box-office man closed his little kiosk and toddled off up on to the promenade where the passing crowds paused for a free look at the show.

'Penny in the box,' I could hear him screeching,

rattling his big, wooden collecting box. 'Small dona-
tions for the Vaudesques gratefully received. Pass
along, please, if you don't wish to contribute.'

As soon as he was gone, I was out of my seat in the
back row – those green, metal, folding chairs with strips
of wood on the seats used to leave weals on my bum –
and nipping into a cosy deck-chair in one of the front
rows, my legs tucked up under so he'd never notice me
when he returned to his kiosk to count the afternoon's
takings.

'What did the brassière say to the top hat?'

'I don't know. What did the brassière say to the top
hat?'

'You go on ahead – I'll give these two a lift!'

'I don't wish to know that. Kindly leave the stage.'

My mother would have gone up the wall if she had
known I was thriving on such filth!

'A medley of your favourite George Formby songs,'
announced the pianist, his reedy voice blown hither and
thither on the fresh breeze which lifted the blue ruffle of
his pierrot costume up round his ears. With his frizzy
ginger hair and his orange make-up he looked like a
portrait of the first Queen Elizabeth.

   'In my profession I work hard, but I'll never stop –
   I'll climb this blinkin' ladder 'til I get right to the top.'

I sang. The man in a straw boater in front of me turned
round and glowered. I shut up and left it to the pianist. I
couldn't risk getting chucked out.

The tall thin one, who looked a bit like Jack Buchanan, did a sort of Fred Astaire-Ginger Rogers routine
with the utterly delectable Valerie Vane who had been a
member of the Vaudesques ever since I had first discovered them and with whom I had been deeply in love
all that time. I slept one whole summer with her
autographed photograph under my pillow.

I was so jealous of the Jack Buchanan type I would have fought him for the right to dance with MY Valerie – if I'd been about ten years older and three feet taller.

And then it was time for Val Vaux's final fifteen-minute solo spot. Talk about Max Miller! He was Max Miller and Arthur Askey and Robb Wilton all rolled into one.

''Allo, 'allo, 'allo. Is everybody happy? You are? Right, we'll soon put a stop to that! Is there anybody here from Swindon?'

'Yes,' yelled half the audience – me included.

'Well, that's your bad luck!'

And all too soon, it was over. And my Trip Day had suddenly lost its sparkle. I shambled away along the prom with many a backward glance at the empty stage and the deserted deck-chairs – back to the bosom of the family and more fish-paste sandwiches and jugs of tea and our kid getting his bottom smacked for jumping on my sister's sand-castle and Gran moaning about her feet and Uncle Tom snoring his head off and Dad looking like Pop-eye with his pipe jutting out of the corner of his mouth and a knotted handkerchief protecting his bald patch from the feeble rays of the late afternoon sun.

'What time's our train go?' demands Gran who always got more excited about going home than going out.

Our kid starts crying.

'I don't wanna go home.'

That starts my sister off.

'If you two don't shurrup, I'll take the pair o' you an' drop you off the end o' the pier!' threatens Dad. 'Look at your brother – he's not yowlin'.'

As a matter of fact, I was just gliding on to the stage of the London Palladium in top hat and tails with Valerie Vane clinging to my arm, dressed in a shimmering red evening gown, while the King and Queen stood in the Royal Box and applauded.

'Wanna see Punch an' Judy an' Toby the dog an' the crocodile an' the 'angman,' my sister demands.

'You've seen 'im three times,' says Mum. 'Anyway, 'e's gone 'ome for 'is tea.'

'No, 'e ain't,' says our kid, stirring it as usual. ''E's on again at 'alf-past five.'

'You an' your great mouth!' Mum slings a tin spade which would have probably decapitated him except that our Mum's got the worst throwing arm in the world.

'Reckon as 'ow it's time we was makin' tracks,' murmurs Uncle Tom the peace-maker. ''Ad a nice day, Ethel?'

'Yes, ta,' says Auntie Ethel, who seems to have done nothing all day except comb the sand out of her hair and touch up her lips with a common, vermilion lipstick. No class, Auntie Ethel – not like Valerie Vane.

'Ow!' shrieks Dad. 'These blasted deck-chairs!'

'Same finger?' enquires Uncle Tom, sympathetically.

He and Dad carry the deck-chairs up the beach and sling them on the pile.

A search begins for Gran's shoes.

Mum starts stowing away all our gear in the push-chair. (I reckon my Mum could pack more in that push-chair than Pickford's men could get in a pantechnicon!)

'Goodbye, seaside,' murmurs our kid, a tear standing on his sandy cheek like a small oasis in a desert. 'See you nex' year.'

'Goodbye, Valerie Vane,' I breathe. 'Please be 'ere nex' year. I'll be thirteen by then.'

''Ere,' says Uncle Tom, coming out of the sweet-shop with a stick of rock for each of us three kids. 'Don't say I never gives you nothin'.'

Somewhere between the prom and the station Uncle Tom and Mr Pinnock and Dad disappear. When they catch up with us Mr P. is belching and burping, Uncle Tom gets ticked off by Auntie Ethel because he's got spots all down the front of his cream cricket shirt, and Dad is all soft-eyed and pink-cheeked and breathing goodwill and beer fumes over everyone.

''Ow about me?' snivels Gran. 'Nobody never thinks about me.'

'Give us 'alf a chance an' I'd never think o' you again as long as I live,' says Dad, shoving a bottle of stout into her hand.

'Fancy that! 'E remembered,' says Gran. As if my lovely Dad ever forgot anybody!

'Come on, then,' yells Mum. 'Ain't any o' you boozy lot gonna give me a 'and with this push-chair?'

And then we're off, with me and our kid hanging out of the window by our toes until the station fades from view behind a curtain of smoke, and the train, like a horse scenting its stable, sets her sights for home and the peace of the engine shed.

'Anybody want a fish-paste sandwich?'

'I'll be sproutin' fins if I as much as see another fish-paste sandwich,' laughs Uncle Tom.

''Ad a nice day, Mr Pinnock?'

'Not bad, I s'pose – as far as it goes.'

''Ow's your stout, Gran?'

'Flat,' grumbles Gran, draining the bottle dry.

'Oh! I do like to be beside the seaside,' sings Dad, a bit tipsy, but by then most of us have dozed off.

'Come on, then,' yells the porter on Swindon Station. 'Ain't you lot got no 'omes to go to?'

We tumble out of the carriages in hundreds, sleepy-eyed, tousle-headed, niggly, scruffy and unutterably sad. All except Gran, of course.

[22]

'Can't wait to get 'ome an' 'ave a decent cup o' tea.'

Dad carries our kid in his arms like a baby, dead to the world, while Uncle Tom, understanding how I feel, walks along with an arm round my shoulder. Mum and Auntie Ethel step it out ahead, Mum as ever behind the push-chair and Ethel patting down her wind-swept perm. Somewhere in the rear, Gran and Mr Pinnock are bringing each other home.

'Cheeroh, Mr Pinnock. See you next Trip.'

'G'night, Uncle Tom. 'Ope your shirt washes out clean.'

The front door slams behind us and the twelfth Trip Day of my life is ended.

Mum undresses the two young 'uns without either of them twitching an eye-lid and Dad swings their little inert bodies over his shoulders like two sacks of coal and carries them off to bed.

'Lovely cup o' tea, this,' purrs Gran, sitting in her armchair, supping, in her stockinged feet with her flowery hat still clamped down over her ears. 'Dawlish nex' year. Get a good cup o' tea at Dawlish.'

''Ad a nice day?' Mum asks, yawning.

'Not bad,' I answer. 'Not bad at all.'

'Say g'night to your Gran, then.'

'G'night, Valerie,' I breathe, kissing Gran on the lobe of her left ear.

'G'night, who?'

'G'night, Mum.'

The stairs stretch ahead of me like Jacob's ladder – up and up to my bedroom in the sky, but I know I'll be all right when I get there because my autographed photograph of Valerie Vane is waiting for me as well as the soft, cool sheets and the certain knowledge that in only three hundred and sixty-four days it will be another Trip Day.

Up the Crossing

Many's the day I've been up the crossing and seen five Castles and three Kings in the space of not much more than half an hour. Not to mention the Halls, the Courts, the Manors, the Bulldogs – and the vast assortment of unnamed goods engines – like the 2-6-0s, the pannier tanks and the hulking great 2-8-0 Consolidations. Like my Gramp used to say – 'Anybody that's never seen the Cheltenham Flyer come leapin' an' roarin' under the first bridge – that's never been wrapped in a grey-black shawl of engine smoke – that's never seen a double-header snortin' an' slippin' at the signal tryin' to take off wi' a 'undred an' more waggons – they've missed some o' the joy in life.'

I reckon he was dead right, too. How can you get excited about a diesel electric? As hygienic as a plastic bag and about as interesting. The sort of engine you could drive wearing your Sunday suit.

I feel sorry for the kids today – I mean, not being able to go up the crossing like we used to do and breathe nothing but choking smoke and warm steam and oil smells all day long. That summer of thirty-eight was something special.

We would set off about ten in the morning with a

day's supply of fish-paste sandwiches and our engine-name-books and stubs of pencil pinched from school. Georgie carried his rations in a brown paper carrier bag; Albie had his sister's tatty old school satchel slung round his neck; Spud's food would be wrapped in a sheet of greaseproof paper and tied up with string, and he always carried it stuffed up his jersey so he had his hands free for emergencies; I lugged along a battered, fraying attaché case which I had found in my Dad's allotment shed and which was secured with a red-and-white-striped trouser belt because the rusted lock had long since given up functioning.

But the envy of us all was Vic. He always led the way – I can see him now, his Gran-knitted grey socks slipping down his calves as he strode out ahead of the rest of us. We would shuffle along a few paces behind him, our eyes taking in every detail of the passing scene, yet always coming back to rest enviously on the brown canvas bag swinging so proudly from Vic's shoulder.

For that bag had travelled on more trains than any of us had seen sunrises. It had belonged to Vic's Gramp. And Vic's Gramp had been a top link guard. He'd risen from being a shunter down the con yard, first to a goods guard and then a passenger guard. He had been on duty on six Royal Trains and had actually shaken hands with the King. I wondered what the King thought of Vic's Gramp's bag!

I'd seen plenty of guards on their way to and from the junction station with their bags slung from their shoulders, their red and green flags poking out from under the flaps. To actually own a real guard's bag like Vic had – to have a Gramp who had travelled on all the top express trains all over the GWR – it wasn't fair really! And my Gramp only a boiler-maker!

Vic's bag looked as old as his Gramp. It had a genuine

oil stain on one side and some different coloured stitching where Vic's Gran had repaired the shoulder strap many times. It was faded and creased and greasy and altogether a most beautiful bag, a genuine railway-man's bag. Vic's sandwiches even tasted better than ours, as if the very smoke and steam and oil and coal-dust of forty years had seeped into the bread itself.

It was a two-mile trek to the crossing along a main road. But once we got to the slaughter-house and climbed the fence into the field that led to the railway track, the world of streets and pavements, petrol-driven cars and horse-drawn carts, houses and schools, parents and teachers and all the other trivia of life were put behind us. Ahead lay the gleaming tracks, parallel pairs of dull metal rails polished to a sparkling silver by a million speeding wheels.

'Come on!' Vic would yell the second we were over the fence and in sight of the engines. 'Let's get a good place on the bank afore the Chapel Street gang gets 'ere.'

We raced for the gently sloping cutting close to the main up line.

'We'll jus' be in time for the ten thirty-six Pad,' puffed Spud, his fat legs scuttling through the mowing grass. As if in answer, a distant whistle from the junction station signalled the departure of the ten thirty-six non-stop express train to Paddington.

'Bet it's Windsor Castle pullin' it,' chirruped Albie.

'Bet yer a pound,' I said.

'You mus' know somethin' if yer bettin' more money than you've ever owned,' said Vic.

'How d'you know it won't be Windsor Castle?' asked Albie.

'Cos she's been in the sheds for repairs all week an' she ain't done a trial run yet,' I announced proudly.

(Having a Gramp who was a boilermaker could be useful sometimes!)

'I reckon it'll be Berry Pomeroy,' said Georgie.

'If I've seen Berry Pomeroy once I've seen 'er an 'undred times,' moaned Albie. 'I 'ope it's one I ain't seen afore.'

'I've seen all the Castle class,' I said, swanking. 'I'm seein' most Castles for the 'undredth time.'

We snuggled down in the long, July grass only a few feet from the up main – near enough to almost feel the power and energy of the great driving wheels as Berry Pomeroy and twelve coaches roared by, building up speed for her seventy-seven-mile journey to London.

We lay in our nest in the grass for a couple of hours – watching express trains and milkies and goods and shunting engines adding their contributions of noise and smell and excitement to the joy of a summer morning – and occasionally enjoying a bit of a scrap among ourselves to keep the blood moving.

'Hey, there!'

A voice, distant yet urgent. A grown-up, man's voice, the sort that sets small boys running away without stopping to ask what they've done wrong. We crouched low in our hide-out. My mind ran expertly through the possibilities. The farmer because we'd trodden down his mowing grass? A railway copper because we were trespassing? The shopkeeper from down the road where Vic had put a ha'penny in the Beechnut chewing-gum machine and thumped it with his fist to try and make two packets come out at one pull?

'Hey there, you kids!'

The voice sounded more imploring than angry now – like my Dad when he wanted me to run over the Co-op and get him twenty cork-tipped.

[27]

I peered over the grassy parapet like an infantryman weighing up the enemy position. A fat man in an apron and a straw boater was standing over the far side of the field, waving his arms and hollering.

'What's up wi' 'im?' muttered Vic, close to my left ear.

'Dunno,' I answered. 'Looks as if 'e's 'avin' a fit!'

Then we saw the other occupant of the field. A black and white dappled horse was prancing through the long grass, heading straight for the crossing. 'Stop 'im! Stop 'im!' yelled the distant fat man. 'E'll kill 'isself!'

Kill 'isself he certainly would if he trotted on to the permanent way with about four expresses and any number of goods trains due along in the next few minutes.

Vic, who was supposed to lead our gang, made no move. Nor did any of the others. They were probably thinking. Very slowly. But this was a time for action, not thoughts. Or perhaps I was the only one who wasn't too scared of horses.

Anyway, I upped and dashed along the embankment towards the spot where the horse looked as though it would career on to the tracks. I began yelling, just any old thing that came into my head.

'Whoa! Get back! Stupid animal!'

The horse ignored me. I tried to run faster, but the long grass imprisoned my legs. I yelled louder and waved my arms around like a small, mobile windmill. The horse cantered steadily on, looking neither to right nor to left. It must have been about fifty yards from the crossing when I saw the banner of white smoke signalling the fast up-milk. I slithered down the embankment on to the rough ballast and began running along the sleepers – the bits that stuck out at the side of the rails. I saw the horse teetering on the brink of the downward slope, pawing the long grass to find a footing. A quick glance ahead at the round, black blob of approaching engine with its halo of smoke and steam, and I was off the sleepers and dashing towards the bank. The horse was tipped forward at a crazy angle as it gingerly felt its way down.

'Get back, boy! Whoa, there!' My voice had to compete with the clanking and chuffing of the 4-6-0 loco.

'Wait there, boy! I'm coming!'

I picked up a handful of ballast and hurled it at the horse's front legs. It spattered in the grass and he hesitated. Another handful smacked him in the chest and he backed up a pace or two. The up-milk let out a fearful shriek as it clattered past, though whether the whistling was a sign of anger towards a small boy on the line or of warning to the horse, I shall never know. Anyway, the horse, suddenly petrified by the din of the rumbling milk wagons, stood his ground. Before I had to make the momentous decision whether to try to catch him by his bridle, cowboy fashion, the fat man arrived and did it for me.

'Never know 'im do nothin' like it, not in all the six years I've 'ad 'im,' the fat man confided, taking off his straw hat to wipe the globs of sweat from his forehead. 'The times I've let 'im out o' the shafts in that very spot so's 'e could 'ave a stretch an' a bite o' fresh grass. Dunno what got into 'im today, I don't.'

But I wasn't listening to him particularly. I was enjoying every bounding moment of my first-ever ride on the driver's seat of a delivery cart. *Johnson's Fresh Fish Delivered to your Door Daily*.

'D'you want a ride?' the fat man had asked me when we got the horse safely re-attached to his cart.

I was too overcome to reply. I just put one foot on the

iron step and was up on the seat in a flash. Vic and Albie and the rest of 'em watched wide-eyed with envy, as I rode off like the Lord Mayor in his coach. They were welcome to their engines today. I had moved into the world of horses.

'You want to drive?' the fat man said, quite casually, as if he was asking me if I liked liquorice.

'Me! Drive!'

''Ere!' He handed me the reins. 'Don't choke 'im,' he added as I gripped the leather straps like a drowning man clutching at straws. 'Just a touch to make 'im go right an' left an' a flick to make 'im shift 'isself, tha's all!'

I drove that horse and cart right through the centre of town, sitting up there like Lord Muck, erect and proud outside and trembling with fear inside. Right down Fleet Street and Farringdon Road we went, in and out of lorries and vans and bikes, with me in charge and my travelling companion exchanging greetings with all the bread-van drivers and milk-float pushers and Walls' ice-cream tricycle-men.

'Why don't you get yourself a decent 'orse?' he yelled at the Co-op delivery man. 'That thing o' yourn looks as if he died a fortnight ago!'

'Morning, officer,' he greeted the policeman by the Town Hall, touching his straw hat in a mock salute.

'Mornin', Wally,' answered the constable. 'Who's the whipper-snapper, then?'

I bent low over the reins for fear he should recognise the whipper-snapper as one of the criminals he had chased along the canal tow-path a few days back for riding three on a bike!

'What d'you think o' this little feller-me lad, eh?' said Wally to the other men in Johnson's Fish Emporium when we drove into the yard. 'Saved our Snowball 'ere from bein' churned into cats' meat by the up-milk, he

[30]

did.' He gave Snowball a sledgehammer pat with one huge, red, fishy hand while lifting me down from my perch with the other. 'What we gonna give 'im, then, for a reward? The fishmonger's Victoria Cross?'

He chortled happily away while we put Snowball in his box and then he led me to his office at the back of the shop.

'What d'you think o' that, then?'

He threw open the door and stood back to watch my face. My eyes nearly popped out of my head. I don't quite know what I expected to see, but I certainly didn't think it would be a railway museum. The walls were covered with photos of engines and old time-tables and posters advertising holidays at far-away GWR places like Newquay and Teignmouth and Tenby. There were books about railways scattered over the desk and piled up in the corners of the room. On the mantelpiece was a model of King George V, perfect scale, about two feet long.

'Jus' 'cos I drive a fish-cart don't mean I don't know nothin' about engines,' he said, shoving me into the room. 'I was train spotting up the crossin', where you was this mornin', years afore you was ever thought of.'

'Who made that?' I breathed, unable to take my eyes off the miniature King George V.

'My Dad,' said Wally, proudly. 'An' not only did 'e make it, 'e drove it. The real one, I mean.'

'Your Dad drove King George V?' I gasped, all incredulous. Fancy me talking to a man whose Dad drove the immortal King!

'Dozens o' times. Prob'ly 'undreds, in fact. Till 'e retired jus' last year.'

I dragged my eyes away from it and inspected the rest of this Aladdin's cave.

'What d'you fancy then?' asked Wally, settling himself on the corner of the huge wooden desk. "'Cept King George, o' course. I wouldn't trade 'im for a hundred Snowballs.'

My gaze had settled on another object, lying in the corner almost buried under a pile of railway magazines. It was dusty and dented – and utterly desirable.

'Could I – I mean, would you –' Unable to ask for it in so many words I pointed at the black, tin box.

'You know a good 'un when you sees it.' Wally tossed the pile of magazines to the floor and swung the metal box up on to the table. 'That's 'is actual box – me Dad's I mean. Seen a few footplates, 'as that one. I dunno 'ow I'm going to part with it, but seein' as 'ow I said you could pick what you fancied . . .'

I honestly reckon there was a tear in his eye as Wally handed over my prize. Looking back, I don't know whether I should have accepted it – but I did.

Next morning, the gang were knocking at our back door before I'd half finished me shredded wheat wanting to know how I'd got on driving the horse and cart yesterday. They all had their paraphernalia ready for another day up the crossing. Albie with his satchel round his neck – Georgie lugging his brown paper carrier bag – Spud with a lump of sandwiches up his jersey – and Vic, of course, standing there swanking with his Gramp's bag slung on his shoulder.

'Shan't be a jiff.' I yelled from the back scullery. 'Jus' packin' me grub.'

''Aven't the bottom fell out o' that ole attaché case yet?' chortled Vic. 'You'll 'ave to find summat else to carry your grub in soon.'

'I 'ave!' I said, stepping out of the back door with more swank in my little finger than Vic had in all his scrawny body.

They fell back against the coal-bunk, goggle-eyed.

'It ain't – not – not a real one, like?' breathed Spud.

'It couldn't be,' muttered Albie, running his hand over the metal lid. 'Could it?'

Vic knew the real thing when he saw it, though. It took him about a minute to get over the shock, then he sidled up to me – he was a nice kid, really, was Vic. 'Who did it b'long to?' he asked.

The others crowded in to hear.

'The driver of King George V.'

'It never did!'

'Honest! Cross me 'eart.'

I licked my index finger and made a solemn cross over the left side of my chest. There was no arguing against that in our gang.

'I'll let you 'ave a taste o' me sandwiches later on,' I said magnanimously. 'I took me chips up to bed in it las' night. They 'ad a real footplate taste to 'em!'

From then on I walked in front, swinging my driver's lunch box for all the world to see. Vic shuffled along behind, his Gramp's bag hanging limply from his shoulder.

All the Fun of the Fair

'Roll up! Roll up! Roll up!' bellowed the man wearing the gold crown and red blazer. ''Ere I am agen, friends – large as life an' twice as natural! I am the Chocolate King. The greatest! The original! The only! Chocolate King!'

'C'mon,' said Albie, 'may as well see what 'e've got this year.'

'Same as las' year,' scoffed Vic. 'Same as ev'ry year.'

'My Dad says it's all rubbish what 'e sells,' said Spud, very serious. 'Else 'e couldn't afford to do it – not at that price.'

'Let's go an' 'ear 'im,' I said, leading the way past the swing boats and the dodgems, between the coconut shies and the Noah's Ark, through the milling, surging crowds, to where the Chocolate King had set up his stall. 'I could listen to 'im for ever.'

To tell the truth, there wasn't a single sound on the fairground that wasn't music to my young ears. And still is! The throbbing power of the traction engines – the hoarse bellowing of the barker outside the boxing booth – the plaintive cries of the old women on the coconut shies and the hoop-la stalls – the Punch and Judy man – the silvery, wind-blown strains of the brass band – the hurdy-gurdy tunes of a dozen competing roundabouts – all mixed up with the joyous chatter and laughter of a thousand happy people.

'Look 'ere! Watch very careful! The speed of the 'and deceives the eye,' proclaimed the Chocolate King, flourishing a big, white, paper bag. ''Ere we go, then. Ev'rybody ready? One box o' peppermint creams. One bar o' fruit an' nut. One bar o' dentists' delight – chocolate covered toffee-de-luxe. Two extra large bars o' creamy, milk chocolate. One bar o' French nougat. And . . .' he paused; then produced a tiny bar of chocolate which he perched on top of the overflowing white bag.

'One on top for the baby!' shrieked the crowd.

'You been 'ere before,' said the Chocolate King, mock serious.

'So 'ave you,' Vic yelled back.

''Ere,' said the Chocolate King, throwing Vic a toffee. 'Take that for your cheek!'

His assistant was busy piling up white bags full of chocolates like the one the King himself had just filled.

''Ow much for this lot?' roared His Majesty. 'There's five bob's worth there if there's a penn'orth. An' 'ow much am I askin'? Not five bob – not even four bob. By the 'eck, I'm robbin' meself today! Three bob. 'Ow's that? No? All right, then, you miserable lot, make it 'alf-a-crown. C'mon, I gotta make a livin'. 'Alf-price it is. What's up, then, all got your pockets sewn up or summat? 'Ere, tell you what. Seein' as 'ow this is the las' time I'll be able to afford to come here, I'll give 'em away! Two bob. Two bob the bagful!'

He smashed his fist down on the counter. Everybody knew they'd have to fork out two bob in the end – they had their florins ready in their hands. They pressed forward and threatened to overturn the stall.

[35]

'I am the Chocolate King,' he sang out as we turned away, disconsolate, our fists buried deep in our empty trouser pockets. 'You can trust your Chocolate King.'

'Swizzle,' Spud said. 'Proper swizzle. All foreign stuff my Dad says. All rubbish.'

'I wouldn't 'ave minded a bar of that nougat even if it is French,' sighed Albie. 'I'm starvin'.

'You can't be,' Vic admonished him. 'You only just 'ad yer cake.'

At the big fête of the year – the third and last of the summer fêtes in the GWR Park – you got real value for money. Threepence to go in and that included a fruit cake in a greaseproof bag and a ticket for a free ride on any roundabout up to four o'clock.

'That was hours ago,' Albie moaned. 'Watchin' 'im an' 'is chocolate's made me 'ungry again.'

'Let's go an' see the Punch an' Judy,' I said, to take his mind off food.

'I only likes Punch an' Judy at the seaside,' he replied. 'They're never no good 'cept at the seaside.'

'This one ain't bad,' Vic put in. ''E can do a proper Punch voice.'

'But 'e ain't got a dog Toby,' said Spud, darkly. And that was that. No self-respecting Punch and Judy man could expect our support if he hadn't got a real, live, dog Toby.

'I think I'm goin' back an' stand by the traction engines for a bit,' I said, diffidently.

'You bin standin' there pattin' them engines for about two hours already,' said Spud.

'No, I ain't,' I snapped. 'An' even if I 'ave, I could stay there all day. An' all night!'

And I could have, too.

I made my way back to where the five giant traction engines were lined up, under the trees, just inside the

[36]

main gate. Never did I see five of these beautiful monsters all generating together except at the Big Fête. Like living creatures they were to me, all dressed up in their coats of rich, plum-red paint and polished brass.

'You wanna come aboard, sunshine?' The driver grinned down at me, his peaked cap askew, the coal-dust swimming on his cheeks in rivers of sweat.

'Me?' I said, unbelieving.

''Oo else? You bin standin' there long enough. I reckon you're in love with the ole girl!'

He reached out two grimy fists and hoisted me on to the foot-plate. Me! Actually ON a traction engine. After a life-time of standing by, watching, touching, dreaming – there I was, up above the world so high, on board Morning Star. If only my Dad could see me now! If only Albie and Vic and Spud – but they had gone to see if they could get in to see the Bearded Lady without paying. Or the five-legged calf. Or the fire-eater. Or –

'What d'you think of 'er then?'

'Me? Think of 'er?' I struggled to find the right words. 'She – well, I mean – it's – um – it's a long way up off the ground, ennit?'

He roared with laughter.

''Ere,' he said, handing me the shovel. 'Stoke 'er up. An' remember – throw the coal well back in the fire-box.'

I hesitated, not sure whether I had the physical strength for the job.

'Go on, you c'n manage. Not too much at a time. An' don't worry about yer 'ands. I got some oily waste 'ere. Yer mother won't never know.'

'Where you bin?' the others greeted me when I found them outside the Ghost Train hours later. 'You ain't 'alf missed some fun. We got in the boxin' booth for nothin'. Vic found a bit o' loose tent an' we crawled underneath. Three fights we seen. Blood an' everythin'. An' one o' the Co-op milk-men got a quid for lastin' three rounds with the Man Mountain. Only 'ad one tooth knocked out, an' got a quid for it, 'e did! Fancy you missin' it.'

How could I explain to them that I hadn't missed a thing? That I'd been on a short visit to Paradise? They wouldn't believe me. And if they did they'd be jealous and spoil the rest of the day.

'You ain't 'alf dirty,' observed Vic. 'You looks as if you been coal minin'.'

'Yeah, well – so I 'ave – sort of,' I said dreamily, and added quickly, 'you seen that bloke dive sixty feet through the flamin' 'oop into a tank o' water? 'E's doing it again in ten minutes. C'mon.'

The fiery August sun simmered down behind the trees, leaving in its wake a pale, clear sky shot with streamers of red and gold.

'Red sky at night,' crooned Spud. 'We'll be able to go fishin' tomorrow.'

'You're in a bit of a 'urry, ain't you?' Vic said. 'We got a lot o' today still left.'

'I gotta be 'ome afore it gets dark,' Albie said. 'Not yet, I don't mean. But afore it gets real black.'

'Don't be daft, Albie.' I put my arm round his shoulder. I liked him best. 'You can't go 'ome before the fireworks. An' they won't light them till at leas' nine o'clock.'

'Anyway,' Vic put in, 'all the fun starts after dark. Everythin' lit up. An' all the young blokes showin' off to their girls an' tryin' to knock off coconuts. An' it's easy to get in some o' the side-shows for nothin' when it's pitch black round the back o' the tents.'

Albie was torn in two.

'Don't worry, Albie, I'm s'posed to be 'ome by dark,

[38]

too. But they don't really mean it. My Mum'd die o' shock if I ever got 'ome the time she told me! An' if you like,' I added, 'I'll come 'ome with you an' tell 'em you 'ad a accident – jus' a small one – an' it took ages to limp 'ome with me 'olding you up!'

'I'd rather me Mam jus' clouted me than tell 'er all that rubbish,' Albie said, ungratefully. 'All right, then. I'll stay.'

As darkness settled cosily over the fairground and the fairy lights cast their magic spell over everyone, we linked arms and shoved our way along the main avenue for the hundredth time.

'Where we goin'?' Spud yelled.

'Back to the tractions?' I suggested hopefully. 'See 'em all lit up.'

'Coconuts!' said Vic.

'Eh?' we replied politely.

'Coconuts!'

Vic, that bit older and bigger than the rest of us, led us away from the crowds, round by the showmen's caravans and the dark, quiet corners behind the stalls and the sideshows.

'If we're gonna be late 'ome, we gotta take a peace off'rin',' explained Vic. 'Like when our Dad comes 'ome late from the pub, 'e always brings our mam a bottle o' stout!'

'We ain't got no money,' observed Albie unnecessarily.

'Anyway, none of us could knock down a coconut,' I pointed out. 'I seen navvies wi' arms like tree trunks 'ittin' coconuts square on an' smashin' the wooden ball to bits without the coconut even rockin'.'

'It's a swindle,' said Spud. 'My Dad says they put lumps of iron inside the coconuts so as they won't come off!'

'Oo's on about money?' Vic demanded. 'I've forgot what money is! I ran out of it 'bout six hours ago. Ten minutes after we got 'ere! I ain't on about knockin' coconuts down – I'm on about knockin' 'em off!'

We looked at Vic with admiration and awe.

''Ow?' I asked him.

'There's always some layin' around on the grass at the back o' the shies. If you lot 'olds the canvas up a bit I can reach under an' get us one each.'

We got down on our stomachs on the dew-damp grass while the wooden balls thwacked into the canvas sheeting above our heads. Very gingerly, Albie and I lifted a corner of the heavy white canvas.

'I c'n see a big 'un,' croaked Vic, squinting under the gap. ''Long a bit to the left.'

We squirmed a bit to our left like four outsize nocturnal caterpillars. Suddenly, Vic shot out his arm and brought it back clutching a huge coconut by its woolly top-knot.

''Ere, Albie. That's yourn.'

'Crikey, Vic, 'e's a beauty. Ta very much.'

''Long a bit more,' Vic ordered. ''An 'old it up a bit 'igher. I gotta reach a bit farther nex' time.'

'Careful, Vic,' Spud begged. 'Somebody'll see you.'

'Naw!' scoffed Vic. 'I'm too quick for 'em.'

His arm shot out again – but came back unrewarded.

'Can't – quite – get 'im.' His face was buried in the long grass as he strained forward, trying to give his arm an extra couple of inches.

'Dash it all!' he muttered. 'I needs a stick or summat.' As I made a move to obey his order, he added, ''Ang on a tick. One more go.'

This time, as Albie and I heaved our hearts out to make the gap a fraction wider, Vic thrust himself violently forward till his head and shoulders and all disappeared under the flap.

[40]

Thwack! A ball made the canvas bulge and zing just above our heads.

Thwack! And another.

Crack! A different note – no movement of the canvas – and Vic very limp and still.

'My God!' breathed Spud. 'They've gone an' killed Vic!'

Albie and I yanked on Vic's ankles and dragged his limp body out of the danger zone. Although scared of what I might see, I rolled him over and inspected his face in the near darkness. There was no blood, thankfully, but a lump the size of a ping-pong ball over his right eyebrow. Afraid of what I might feel, I shoved my hand down his jersey and placed my palm on the left side of his chest.

'He ain't – y'know, not – well . . .' stammered Albie who was very close to tears, panic and a few other things.

'I can't tell, can I, if you don't shurrup.' I bent and placed my head against Vic's ribs to see if my ear could pick up what my hand had failed to find.

'Put a mirror in front of 'is mouth an' if it goes all steamy, 'e's alive,' breathed Spud. 'I seen 'em do it at the pictures.'

'You gotta mirror?'

'Eh? Well, er, no!'

'What you on about, then?'

I gave up searching for Vic's elusive heart and tried his pulse.

''E's alive,' breathed Spud. 'I seen 'is chest move.'

'That was my 'and comin' out of 'is jersey!'

''E made a noise,' croaked Albie. 'I 'eard 'im. A kind o' groan it was.'

We listened for further intimations that Vic's young life had not been prematurely ended by a misdirected wooden ball.

[41]

''E's only unconscious,' I announced eventually.

''Ow do we get 'im conscious?' asked Albie.

'Throw cold water over 'im?' Spud suggested tentatively.

'We better get a amb'lance man,' I advised.

'Not be'ind 'ere, we can't,' Spud cried. 'They'll wanna know what we was doin'.'

'We can't very well move 'im,' I countered. ''E's too 'eavy to carry an' if we drag 'im 'e might 'it 'is 'ead again on a tent peg or summat!'

The problem was promptly resolved when a hefty great bloke with rolled-up shirt sleeves, and a big stomach hanging over the front of his trousers, nearly fell over us.

'What's all this 'ere, then?' he bellowed. 'What d'you think you're a-doin' of?'

Quick as a flash I nipped in. ''E've 'ad a accident, mister. Tripped over one o' them ropes an' 'it 'is 'ead, 'e 'ave.'

''Ave 'e now,' said the big bloke, kneeling in the damp grass and smoothing Vic's forehead as gentle as Florence Nightingale. 'Better bring 'im in 'ere, then.'

He scooped up Vic's long, skinny torso in his thick, hairy arms and disappeared into the nearest caravan.

'If you lot are comin' in, for Gawd's sake 'urry up. An' when you gets yourselves inside – put the wood in the 'ole be'ind you!'

Never before in my life had I crossed a threshold that led into another world, another way of life. A house on wheels.

No – not a house, a *home!* A fascinating, breathtaking, exotic, complete home in a box twenty feet long and six feet wide. A moving home that could take you – well, anywhere. Towed behind Morning Star! A different fairground every week-end!

[42]

'Looks like Carnera 'it 'im with a straight right,' boomed the man, slopping cold water over Vic's bump.

'Will 'e be OK?' we enquired, gathering round the body, all of us suddenly wide-eyed with fear.

In answer to our question, Vic stirred – and I felt free to return to my contemplation of life in a caravan. I knew how Mr Toad felt in that book our sir had read to us at school.

'Wish you lived in 'er, do you?' grinned the man as my gaze flitted around the van, taking in the neat, red curtains, table lamps, scaled-down furniture, red and gold china plates, potted plants. 'A place for everything and everything in its place,' as my Gran would have said.

'Don't I just!' I breathed. 'I wouldn't never want nothin' else as long as I lived.'

I had always imagined the inside of a showman's caravan being about as comfortable as the shed down the end of our garden. A couple of old chairs, a scruffy table, a bunk bed, a tin plate and a mug, bare floor-boards . . . How wrong can you be? This was the most luxurious home I had ever been in, with or without wheels.

'Take the weight off your legs. 'E won't be ready to go 'ome for a bit.'

We sat down obediently. While he bathed Vic's head he told us stories about life on the fairgrounds.

'Di'n't you oughta be workin' now?' Albie asked.

'I got an hour off,' the man replied, sloshing a bottle of beer into a mug. 'My sons are lookin' after the Big Wheel for an hour. Then I'll be back on till midnight.'

'Where am I?' said Vic, just like they did in films – though I never knew till then people said it in real life.

''E ought to go up the 'ospital,' said the man as Vic tottered to his feet.

[43]

'No, no,' Vic pleaded, 'I'm all right. Really I am.'

'I dunno.' The man stroked his stubbly chin.

'My Mum's a nurse,' lied Vic.

We got ready to leave. I had a last, long look round – trying to paint a picture in my mind which I could keep for ever and take out and look at when I was in bed at night.

'Oh!' squealed Albie. 'I've lost me coconut.'

'Don't tell me you knocked down a coconut,' the man guffawed, squeezing Albie's puny bicep.

'No – er – not exactly,' Albie stalled – then added truthfully, 'somebody gave it to me.'

'Well now, let's see what we got.' The man pulled out a sack from underneath the van. He plunged an arm in and brought out two coconuts. He handed one each to Albie and Vic, then produced two more for Spud and me.

'Ta, mister,' we said, four times, separately. 'Ta very much.'

'One more thing,' he hollered as we disappeared into the night. 'You wanna keep away from be'ind them coconut shies. You could get a nasty knock from one o' them wooden balls!'

The last thing I saw of him he was standing on the steps of that beautiful caravan, guzzling his beer and rocking with laughter.

'I reckon we missed the fireworks,' sighed Albie as a final salvo of rockets exploded overhead in a burst of green and red and gold stars. Above the heads of the vast crowd the huge words, GOODNIGHT CHILDREN, spluttered and faded in a haze of smoke.

'We oughta be goin' 'ome, anyway,' Spud said.

'I wish I was in bed already,' moaned Vic.

We trudged home slowly, clutching our coconuts and our memories. Home in a terraced house would never

[44]

be the same again. Not compared with life in a caravan pulled by a traction engine.

We parted under the street lamp.

'See you tomorrow,' I said.

'If I'm still livin',' Vic sighed.

'Doubt if I'll be allowed out tomorrow,' whimpered Albie. The town hall clock struck eleven. 'Nor all nex' week!' he added.

My mother greeted me with a smart cuff round the ear.

'What time d'you think this is, then?'

'Jus' gone 'leven o'clock,' I suggested – and got another clipped ear for my trouble.

'Your Dad's been searchin' the streets for hours,' she exaggerated. 'You bin to your last fair, you 'ave. Now get off up them stairs.'

'But Mam – Vic 'ad this accident, see. 'E was knocked unconscious an' this man – '

'I don't want none o' your lies,' she chipped in.

'But it's true,' I persisted. 'Honest it is!'

'You an' the truth are total strangers. Now get off to bed afore your father sets about you.'

Half-way upstairs my stomach reminded me of something. 'Mam! I ain't 'ad no supper.'

'Nor you ain't gettin' none, either.'

'I ain't 'ad a wash!'

'It'll keep till mornin'!'

'I brought you a coconut, Mam!'

'If you pinched it, your Father'll murder you!'

I snuggled down between the sheets – warm, grubby, happy. Happy because I knew where I was going one of these days when they got on to me and clipped my ear for nothing. One of these days – not tonight, because I was very tired – but one of these days I'd show 'em. I'd pack my bag and push off where a boy would be welcome, where big, hairy men drank beer out of mugs and kept sacks and sacks of coconuts.

Just before I slid off into sleep, I distinctly felt the bed lurch, heard a faint whistle followed by a *chuff-chuff-chuff* – and we moved off, gently, into the night.

'Name an' Address?'

I sat astride the hoardings at the bottom of the Milk Bank and it was a cracking good world to be alive in. The sky was a cloudless blue. It was still only half-way through the long summer holiday. I was as free as the starlings that fidgeted around the guttering on the signal box. It was one of those languid summer days that we used to enjoy so regularly when we were kids and which we never seem to get nowadays. And it was the first day a policeman ever took out his notebook and asked me the dreaded question: 'What's your name an' address, then?'

Not that I hadn't skirmished with the law before. There had been a couple of clips round the ear for playing football in the street, a few tickings off for riding two (or three – or four!) on a bike, and a fairish number of chases along the canal path for lighting unauthorised bonfires on November the fifth or sniping with pea-shooters on almost any other day of the year. But never before had I been cornered and faced with notebook and pencil.

'You seen Manorbier Castle?' yelled Albie from his perch atop the next hoarding. 'She've got a new name-plate. A straight 'un.'

'Tell us summat new,' I jeered. 'I seen 'er weeks ago.'

'Ennit about time for the up-Fishguard?'

'Keep your eyes skinned. She've been signalled about five minutes.'

From the tops of the hoardings we commanded a superb view of the junction station, the sidings and the main line – Paddington to Bristol and all points west. The hoardings were some twenty feet high and pretty easy to climb on the side facing the tracks. On the other side, facing the station approach road, they were plastered with huge posters bearing great, domino-shaped cubes of Oxo, glasses of velvety-black Guinness, the Bisto Kids and boxes of Bryant and May's matches the size of a baby Austin.

The up-Fishguard came swaying and rattling through the station. Just as the loco was coming up abreast of us – we had our stubs of pencil and notebooks poised to tick off her name – the stopper from Didcot chugged across right in front of her and completely blocked our view.

'Missed 'er!' howled Albie. 'I blinkin' well missed 'er! D'you get 'er?'

'No,' I hollered back, almost swallow-diving to the ground in frustration and anger. 'I think it was a Court.'

'Never! It was a Castle.'

'A Castle! You mus' be blind. 'Er chimney stack was wrong for a Castle.'

'You couldn't tell a Castle from a pannier tank! Any 'ow, I'm goin' 'ome. We got chitt'lin' for dinner.'

'If we 'ad chitt'lin' for dinner,' I said haughtily, 'I wouldn't never go 'ome!'

I watched, disappointed, as Albie clambered down, agile as a monkey shinning down a tree.

'See you later?' I called hopefully.

'I dunno,' answered Albie, trotting away. 'I gotta do some errands for our Mum s'afternoon.'

I watched until his green jersey and patched flannel trousers were a blur on my horizon, and turned back to the trains. I realised, suddenly, how stiff my legs were and how sore my backside was. I'd been astride that chunk of four-inch timber for a solid hour. I eased myself down, hand over hand, and went off to search for trouble in pastures new.

I wandered up the slope of the Milk Bank, past the black and white, cast-iron plate which proclaimed GWR PROPERTY. TRESPASSERS WILL BE PROSECUTED, and bunked myself up on to the little platform that ran the length of the sidings, where they loaded and unloaded parcels and milk churns and other fascinating items of freight.

The platform had been made of old sleepers which had been pensioned off after decades of service on the permanent way. I played a game of seeing how many sleepers I could jump from a standing start; then, how many off a three-pace run. I soon found myself at the far end of the platform, right against the signal box.

Old Joe leaned out of the window of the box, caressed his walrus moustache and greeted me. "'Op it!" he said.

'Can't 'ear you!' I replied cheerfully.

'Cheeky young devil,' shouted Joe – but I fancied there was a hint of a smile tucked away under all those whiskers. 'You'll catch it if Sergeant Jones get 'old of yer.'

'Go on back to your signals,' I shouted. 'Else you'll 'ave the Cheltenham Flyer an' the Bristolian an' about six coal trains shuntin' each other up their guard's vans!'

Joe slammed the window, polished his hands with a lump of oily waste and turned his attention to the signalling business.

The sound of gently rustling wings and plaintive

cooing drew me over to a large square, wicker basket. I made cooing noises to show that I was a friend. 'Where you goin' to, then?' I bent to examine the label. 'You got a long way to go, ain't you? Dunno where Leeds is 'xactly, but I wish I was comin' with you!'

None of the pigeons appeared interested in holding any sort of conversation so I addressed myself to a lump of coal which had fallen off one of the shunting engine's tenders and thus saved itself from instant cremation in a fire-box. It was shiny and smooth – best Welsh steam coal – about the size of a cricket ball and just begging to be kicked.

I kicked it.

I hit a round, metal drum full of something or other.

It made a rich, ringing clonk.

I recovered it and had another shot. I scored eight hits out of ten.

'Very good,' said a sarcastic voice behind me, which lifted me clean off my feet with surprise. 'Quite a little Dixie Dean, ain't we?'

My first reaction was that of any criminal, prisoner-of-war or cornered rat – to search for an escape route.

There was none.

Well, there was one, to be exact. A four-foot plunge on to the tracks, and instant suicide under the wheels of a shunting engine!

There didn't seem to be any need to go that far – yet!

Sergeant Jones of the Railway Police was what my mother would have called 'a fine figure of a man'. The sort of man who blocked out your entire view of the sky when he stood in front of you. And there he was, standing in front of me and – oh, God, please, not that – unbuttoning his top pocket and – it can't be true, please, oh please let it be a dream – taking out his notebook!

[50]

'But – but – I ain't done nothing!' I stammered.

'You're trespassing,' snapped the law. 'And it's not the first time, neither.' He flipped open the book.

'It is!' I lied, desperately. 'I di'n't know it was trespassing! Honest I didn't. I won't do it again.'

'That's a fact you won't,' said Sergeant Jones, licking the point of his indelible pencil. 'I'm gonna make a hexample of you. What's your name an' address, then?'

I seriously considered the suicide bit. Actually, I couldn't have found my way to the edge of the platform because of the blinding tears that filled my eyes.

'C'mon, c'mon. You heard me. Name an' address, or do we go over to the stationmaster's office?'

My mother would kill me. But I wasn't too bothered about that. It was my Dad. He'd lose his job. If I was had up in front of the beak for breaking the railway company's law, then my Dad would be kicked out of that same company's workshops. 'Any excuse,' my Dad used to say. 'Any excuse, they'll sack you.' And they'd have to sack a man, no matter how long his service or how clean his record, if he had a son – a criminal son – who had so far transgressed the GWR law as to trespass on its property.

'You struck dumb or somethin'?' He took my skinny shoulder in his iron fist and shook me till I thought I would fall apart at the seams.

Automatically, I spelled out my surname for him. We all do it in our family. It's such an unusual name, nobody can ever spell it. There's only one lot of us, according to my Gramp. 'You meet anyone with our name,' he used to say. 'They'll sure to be related.'

Sergeant Jones paused, frowned, licked his pencil so violently he painted a purple streak down his tongue.

'What was that? Spell it again,' he demanded. Did he think I was pulling a false name on him? Who could invent a name like ours?

[51]

''S true,' I said. 'That's my real name.'

'Where d'you live?'

I hesitated.

'It'll be the worse for you if you tell me any whoppers.'

I told him.

He wrote slowly, thoughtfully, while the tears burned channels down my cheeks and I wondered if he was about to caution me – *anything you say may be taken down and used in evidence –*

Instead, he said, 'You got any hanties?'

'Hanties?'

'Yes, hanties. You've 'eard of hanties and huncles!'

'Oh! Well, yes – I got lots.'

'You got a Hanty Hethel?'

'Yeah. I got an Auntie Ethel.' Two or three, in fact. I looked into his face and noticed for the first time that he was a human being in disguise.

He cocked his big round head to one side and said: 'Where d'she work?'

'Exeter.'

'On the railway?'

'Well, she ain't an engine driver!' My sense of humour was recovering from the shock, but when I saw he didn't think much of the joke, I added quickly: 'She's manageress in the station refreshment rooms.'

I could have bitten my tongue off the minute I'd said it. Now they'd not only give my Dad his cards but my Auntie Ethel as well. I could see our whole family on the dole – blacklisted by every railway company – my chance of being taken on as an apprentice gone for ever.

'Please,' I begged, 'couldn't you give me a wallopin'? Or a clip round the ear'ole? Or – or – summat?'

He snapped the book shut, carefully put it away and very slowly buttoned up his pocket. 'Push off 'ome,' he

[52]

said, turning on his size twelve heel and striding off up the platform.

'But – but – what's goin' to 'appen to me?'

'You'll see soon enough,' he boomed.

Walking home, I understood for the first time how King Charles must have felt, taking that final walk to the chopping block. I stumbled along on inadequate legs, my mind like a dollop of scrambled egg, not quite sure whether to share my guilty secret with the family or stew in lonely silence until the day when the official envelope would thump on to the front door mat, inviting me to attend the juvenile court up Old Town police station. I decided, with my usual cowardice, to allow them all to live on in their fool's paradise. 'Sufficient unto the day,' my Gramp would have said. He was full of sayings.

'You're late! Your dinner's in the dustbin,' my mother welcomed me. 'You've gone an' tore them trousers again. An' jus' look at the colour o' your knees! You bin crying or summat? You ain't bin down the wharf an' got me coal ticket yet.'

I went out in the back yard and sat in the shed all the afternoon.

'Where've 'e gone now,' I heard my Dad saying. 'Never find that blasted kid when you wants 'im. Thought 'e was goin' over the co-op an' get me some fags.'

About seven o'clock I reappeared. My stomach was as hollow as a base drum and making noises like I was having a private, internal thunderstorm.

'You ain't 'ad a bite to eat all day. You ill or summat?'

The table was as bare as Mother Hubbard's cupboard and the cloth was put away.

'I've cleared and washed the tea things. There's a doughnut in the bread bin if you want. An' 'urry up an'

[53]

get them knees washed an' put your bes' trousers on. Your Auntie Ethel'll be 'ere soon.'

I'd clean forgot Auntie Ethel was coming. She came every fourth Saturday. On the four o'clock from Exeter, change at Bristol, leaving the refreshment rooms to the assistant manageress until she got back late Sunday night.

She was my Dad's youngest sister. She had no home – only a poky little room over the station. I never had been able to figure out why she wasn't married. She was pretty and wore smart clothes and told funny stories and always brought chocolate for me and our kid, and she knew plenty of engine drivers.

'You'll be goin' to the station to meet 'er,' said Dad.

How could I tell him I never wanted to see another station again as long as I lived?

'It'll be too late by the time I've washed,' I said.

'There's 'er case to be carried.'

'You better go yourself, Dad,' my mother said.

'Me leg's playin' up summat chronic.' My Dad put on his heroic look and laid his leg across the fireside stool as if it was made of wood.

'Comes in very 'andy at times, does your leg,' my mother snapped. 'Prob'ly feel better if Ethel wants you to take 'er down the pub later on!'

I don't think my Mum was as fond of Ethel as I was. I was devoted to her – and not only because of the chocolate.

'I'll go an' meet Auntie Efful,' piped up our kid, looking like a junior type angel with his pink ears, blue eyes, blonde curls and soppy little tweed suit. I could have punched his smug face.

'You're a good 'un,' my mother purred, patting his head. 'But you're not big enough to go on your own, not yet awhile.'

[54]

She glared at me. Oh crumbs! I thought, that's nothing to the way she's going to look when she hears how I've brought the family reputation crashing around our feet. 'Once you've lost your good name – you've lost everythin',' gramp would have said.

I returned to my lonely contemplations in the shed – armed with a doughnut from the bread bin. The one with the most gluey, blood-red raspberry jam oozing out of its sugary coat. Well, I mean, there was no point in starving to death. Not yet. We'd be doing that soon enough when my Dad got kicked out of the company.

I heard the front door bell ring, followed by scurrying footsteps and yelps of greeting. I laid my head on my Dad's workbench – made out of a barrowload of GWR scraps, bought and delivered for sixpence ¬ and I cried all over the spanners and chisels and screwdrivers.

'I dunno where ·'e've gone,' I heard my mother explaining. ''E's in a right stroppy mood today.'

And there was my Dad chatting in the background – and another man's voice answering him.

My mother and Auntie Ethel came out into the back yard. They often did if they had secret things to talk about that they didn't want my Dad or us kids to overhear.

''Ow long you known 'im?' my Mum was saying.

'Long enough,' said Ethel, giggling. She had a lovely giggle, it fairly sparkled with inner happiness.

'You ain't – well, I mean – y'know, goin' steady?' My mother had her nosy voice on.

'We might be.' Ethel did a repeat giggle.

'Well!' said Mum. 'I dunno what Dad's goin' to say about that, I'm sure.'

'None of his business. He's only me brother, not me keeper!'

[55]

'Well!' said Mum again.

I could tell that she was proper flabbergasted.

'Thought you 'ad two lads.' I heard the man come out in the yard.

'Go on in, you,' said Ethel. 'This is a private conversation.'

'Pardon me for breathing,' the man laughed.

'I dunno where the other 'un 'ave gone,' said Mum.

Auntie Ethel unlatched the shed door.

'Fancy that,' she said in mock horror. 'First time you've not met me and carried me case for years. Gone off me, have you? Don't want to unpack me case and find what I've brought you?'

'No, no!' I cried. 'I mean – yes. Yes, course I do.' Oh, how I loved diving my hands into the layers of cool, frothy, silky clothes and bringing out bars of Fry's chocolate cream for me and our kid, and Plain York for Mum, and twenty Craven 'A' for Dad!

'Ain't even got a kiss for me, then?' she pouted.

I wasn't all that keen on the kissing bit, even though her cheek was soft and she smelt of Californian Poppy and it wasn't a bit like kissing our Mum or our Gran or our Great Aunt Sarah, who had a prickly, grey moustache and clickety false teeth.

Auntie Ethel bent forward, I hesitated – then lurched forward into her arms like a great, soft baby and pressed my grubby, soggy cheek into her permanent waves.

'Oh! Auntie Ethel,' I sobbed. 'You'll never believe what I've done!'

She stroked my tousled hair and through my tears I saw over her shoulder the smudgy outline of the man.

'Well! Well!' he said.

There was a sort of something that puzzled me. I dried my eyes in Auntie Ethel's hair.

'What's the matter with my little man?' she was

[56]

whispering in my ear. 'C'mon, you can tell your Auntie Ethel –'

'Great, soft cry-baby,' snorted Mum.

'How's the champion train spotter, then?' said Sergeant Jones.

In his brown suit and without his helmet he looked altogether different – just an ordinary man. Like my Dad, only bigger. Even the timbre of his voice was changed.

'Lost your tongue?' Mum snapped.

'This is Bill,' said Auntie Ethel, disentangling her hair from my face. 'Guess what 'e does for a livin'.'

Me guess? I only wished I needed to guess! And he had to come to the house and shame me in front of everybody – including Ethel.

Still, it had to happen sometime. It would save me having to pluck up courage to tell them – or the interminable wait until the fateful letter arrived from the juvenile court.

''Ere,' said Auntie Ethel, frowning, 'what d'you mean, "your champion train-spotter?" 'Ave you two met?'

'Sure,' Sergeant Jones grinned, disclosing two front teeth to match Bugs Bunny. 'We're both railway men at heart, ain't we, son?'

I nodded like a dumb idiot, not sure what sort of game he was playing.

''E's daft about engines, 'e is.' Mum tossed her head at me. 'If ever I don't know where 'e is, I bet 'e's down them railway sidin's.'

'What the 'eck's goin' on out 'ere?' My Dad came shooting out of the house, suddenly remembered his gammy leg and leaned against the wash-house wall for support. 'Ain't we goin' down the pub an' 'ave a little celebration drink?'

He looked at Auntie Ethel and Sergeant Jones.

'You're always goin' down there to celebrate summat or other,' my Mum said. 'What's so special tonight?'

'Blimey, woman, you blind or summat,' laughed Dad. 'Can't you see 'ow this pair are fixed?'

Auntie Ethel blushed all over her visible parts and whispered in my ear, ''Ow d'you fancy 'im for your new Uncle Bill?'

To my Dad she said, 'Well, it'll be keeping the GWR in the family, won't it? An' bring a bit o' law an' order into this unruly 'ouse'old.'

'Jus' fancy,' my mother said – and it was as if she suddenly liked Auntie Ethel a lot better – 'A p'liceman in the family. Your Gramp would've liked that!'

'What d'you reckon?' Auntie Ethel cocked her head at me. I looked hard at Sergeant Jones. He gave me an enormous wink.

'Smashin',' I said.

Well, I mean, there's a thing in our laws, isn't there, about not being allowed to give evidence against your own relations? Not that Uncle Bill ever seriously meant to report me, did he?

Or did he?

The Sunday School Treat

'Where you goin'?' Albie yelled across the street this particular Sunday morning.

I looked all around before I answered him because it wasn't the sort of thing I wanted all our nosy neighbours to hear.

'Sunday School,' I said in a hoarse whisper.

Albie nearly fell off the dividing wall. 'What!' he croaked.

I hurried on.

'Where you goin' – down the Mission?'

'No,' I muttered. 'St Peter's.'

'Where?' Albie came trotting after me.

'You 'eard. St Peter's.'

'Whaffor? You ain't church. You're chapel.'

'I've changed,' I said loftily.

'Since when?' sneered Albie. 'Las' time you ever went to Sunday School it was down the Mission 'all. An' that was an 'eck of a while ago!'

We walked on in silence – me in front in my best pullover and grey shorts and knee-length knitted socks and shiny new shoes, Albie scurrying along behind in his normal Sunday clobber; grey vest, patched trousers with the seat hanging out, and daps whose uppers and soles had so nearly reached the parting of the ways that they grinned at every step, their open mouths revealing an assortment of sock and toe.

'What you goin' up there for?' he demanded. ''S a long way jus' for Sunday School. The Mission 'all's only up the lane. Or you could go down the Sally Army. They 'as their church 'tween the off licence an' Melias's. I know a kid as goes there.'

'I'm goin' up St Peter's,' I said.

Albie hesitated, then, recognising the finality of my last statement, turned and sloped off back home. I felt a bit bad about it – treating Albie like that – but I didn't really want to discuss this new venture with anybody. Not yet. Particularly not with Albie.

I strode on up the hill, past the cenotaph where a few tatty poppy wreaths still littered the base of the white marble column, past Jackson's where they had the big model engine in the window that Spud reckoned was worth a hundred pounds. (Or did he say a thousand? I know it was the best model engine I'd ever seen and I had to stop just for a couple of ticks to have another gander at it.) Past the Mechanics' Institute, the Town Hall, loads of sweet shops that were all closed – until I came to old Mrs Wicks's.

It was a part of the town I knew hardly at all, but I knew old Mrs Wicks's little shop and the sherbet dabs and liquorice laces and brandy balls and coconut ice and sweet cigarettes and – things. And she stayed open on Sundays! I didn't know for sure if it was against the law but seeing that all the big 'uns closed I thought it was pretty brave of Mrs Wicks to defy them all and open.

I fingered the two pennies in my pocket. They were warm where I had been turning them over in my palm. Two warm pennies. One from my Mum and one from my Gran. ('As long as you're not going to the Methodists!' Gran said. 'I don't hold with them ever since the minister forgot to turn up for your Great Uncle Alfred's funeral and they had to fetch him out of the Co-op restaurant!') Two warm pennies for the cold collection plate. What for? Who got the benefit? Did it help pay the vicar's wages? Or buy those horrible white flowers like giant ear-trumpets that they messed up church altars with? Or did it really go to feed the starving kids in India and Africa and Glasgow and all those other foreign places?

'Be a darn sight better off if they left 'em alone to look after theirselves,' my Dad used to say. 'Goin' sendin' mission'ries an' tellin' all them black people about God when they got plenty o' Gods o' their own. Jus' messes 'em up, that's what I say. Better if we left 'em to choose their own religion.'

He's probably right, I thought. My Dad was often right when he said things like that. I thought it would be perfectly reasonable to share the two pennies between the needs of the church and the needs of my stomach. One penny towards the vicar's dinner or those deathly flowers or those far-away un-Christian people. And a pennyworth out of Mrs Wicks's window. Seemed a fair enough arrangement. I didn't think my Mum and Gran would actually agree – but then they never did see eye to eye with the obvious, logical, sensible way I worked these things out!

I pressed against the grimy bay-window of Mrs Wicks's shop. It was really an ordinary house which had been made into a shop by knocking down the front garden wall and putting a counter in the front room.

The glass struck cold against my nose and finger tips. I studied the assortment of jars and cardboard boxes carefully. I wasn't going to rush it. Probably the best value would be to buy two items at a ha'penny each rather than squander the entire penny on a single luxury. A Beechnut chewing gum *and* a sherbet fountain? Or some aniseed balls *and* a fruity chew? Or half-an-ounce of jelly beans in a three-cornered bag *and* a cream-filled chocolate soldier? Such a problem to be faced so early on a Sunday morning. Financial problems were extremely rare, anyway!

Having changed my mind four times between shoving open the heavy wooden door and seeing the vision that was Mrs Wicks come trundling in from the back room, I finally came out with a bar of Sharp's toffee and a packet of XXX Extra Strong Mints.

The minute I was out on the pavement I wished I'd had a sherbet dab and a gob-stopper, but it was too late. Anyway, if I'd changed I'd have probably finished up wishing I'd stuck to what I'd got in the first place. Life could be very complicated.

I sucked my Sharp's toffee bar all up through the Market Place and round by Marks and Spencer's so I could have a quick, adoring look at Laddie and Lassie. The two fire-engines, the pride and joy of all the kids in the town, altogether too posh for the tumbledown old fire station which housed them. All shiny red paint and gleaming brass.

Round by the Rising Sun and past the King's Arms, both looking desolate and tatty in the quietness of Sunday morning after the hullaballoo of Saturday night.

And there was St Peter's.

Gaunt, grey and totally overwhelming. I thought it must be the biggest building in the town, if not in the whole of England (except for Buckingham Palace and Paddington Station, both of which I had seen on a half-day excursion to London with my Gramp.)

St Peter's stood surrounded by a cemetery full of flying angels and artificial flowers inside glass domes.

Oh Lord, I prayed, don't let me die yet! Not if heaven is full of ugly, baby-faced angels and flowers. I don't want to go there.

I gazed up at the spire and recalled, quite unexpectedly, little Miss Price in the Infants' School telling us Salisbury Cathedral spire was the tallest building in Wiltshire. It must be tall if it's higher than this, I thought, my eyes going all peculiar as the spire threatened to fall on me the longer I stared at it. Perhaps Salisbury Cathedral was also a very large church?

I made my way around the churchyard to the hall which lay beyond, next door to a big house built of the same depressing, grey stone as the church. I supposed the vicar lived there, though I would have had nightmares sleeping in a bedroom whose windows overlooked a vista of tombstones. The hall was much more modern; red brick with nice, square window panes rather than the tall, thin, pointed, stained-glass church windows. After a moment's uncertainty, I pulled my socks up, took a mighty deep breath and pushed open one of the swing doors.

'And where d'you reckon you're going, then?'

I nearly leaped out of my shoes as the deep bass voice boomed in my ear. I turned to inspect the owner of the voice and found that they matched. He was a big man, mostly covered in a black suit, the waistcoat bulging out in front with a heavy, gold watch-chain as its only ornament.

'Can't you speak when you're spoken to?'

His several chins rippled as he spoke. His flabby white hand took a firm grip on my shoulder.

Well, I thought, this is a fine way to welcome a lost sheep. All that talk about people not going to church and Sunday School. No wonder, if this is the sort of greeting you get! 'I wanna join,' I said briefly.

'Oh aye!' the fat man boomed. 'And what, may I ask, do you want to join?'

I nearly said I didn't want to join anything if he was running it. Instead I told him I wanted to be a member of the Sunday School.

'Oh aye! And what suddenly made you come over all religious?'

I hope Heaven hasn't got a gateman like this bloke, because if they have their numbers must be going down fast.

'I thought anybody could go to Sunday school if they wanted to,' I answered bravely, shaking myself free of his pincer hold on my shoulder. 'I di'n't know you 'ad to explain anythin'. I thought your lot was tryin' to get more of our lot to join.'

'Where d'you live?' he asked.

'Down by the station.'

'Why don't you go to All Saints'?'

'I bin there an' I don't like it. An' I bin to the Mission 'all an' the Congs an' the Wesleyans an' —'

'None of them suit your lordship?' he cut in sarcastically.

'I'm tryin' to find what one suits me best,' I lied.

And felt very guilty when I realised I was standing on Holy Ground spouting bare-faced lies. Or perhaps a church hall isn't really holy, not like a church itself? Anyway, it wasn't a terrible lie, not the sort of lie that gets other people into trouble. That's what I call a real black lie. No, this was more a sort of pale grey lie, because in a kind of way I was trying to discover what this new Sunday School had to offer. Though not, perhaps, in quite the way old Fatty, the doorkeeper, would understand.

'You ain't got some little game up your sleeve, have you?' He bent low and scrutinised me closely. I put on

[64]

what I hoped was my best angelic look. It was a bit difficult to keep it up because his breath reeked of tobacco – not a nice, rich, pipe smell like the front of my Gramp's waistcoat gave off, but a horrible, stale, cigarette stink.

'I knows your sort,' he said, straightening up. 'And I'll be keeping an eye on you, don't you fret. So watch your step. Right?'

I nodded.

'How old are you?'

Before I had decided what might be the best age to assume – I could pass for anything between nine and thirteen depending what advantages attached to the particular age group – we were joined by a third person.

At first it seemed a long, thin, black bird had flown in through the swing doors, leaving them sighing and squeaking in his wake.

'Oh!' exclaimed the long, thin, black bird. 'What have we here, then, Mr Perkins? A new lamb come to join our flock?'

'Um – well – er, yes, I s'pose you could say so, vicar,' grunted Mr Perkins rather unwillingly.

The long, thin, black bird – otherwise known to his flock as the Reverend Timothy Trotman – lifted one wing and placed a cold, bony hand on my head.

'How jolly nice. And what might your name be, my little man?'

If it hadn't been for the pressure of his hand on my head, I would have scarpered. My little man indeed! I'd rather people insulted me than that! I mean, well, I was used to insults. From just about everybody.

'Speak up, then, laddie. Haven't lost our tongue, have we?'

Between the Rev Trotman and Mr Perkins I didn't reckon St Peter's deserved any flock. No wonder my

Mum and Dad and Gran had given it all up years ago. They didn't even force me to go any longer. Didn't think it was worth all the rows and upsets, I suppose, trying to turn their son and heir into a particular variety of Christian.

'Now, now, little man, mustn't be afraid, must we? Nobody's going to eat you, eh, Mr Perkins? Don't throw Christians to the lions any more!'

He must have thought that was very funny because he let out a great squawk of a laugh that went quite well with his bird-like appearance.

'I don't know why he don't go to All Saints',' Mr Perkins thundered. 'He lives right over the other side of town.'

'Maybe he feels the long walk will benefit him physically whilst St Peter's can offer him spiritual consolation,' cooed the vicar.

'Huh!' snorted Mr Perkins.

I don't think he understood what the vicar was on about any more than I did.

'How old are you, little man?' The vicar poked his long, pointed nose into my face.

'I asked him that already,' Mr Perkins told him. 'And he don't seem to know. I don't think he's very . . . er . . .' He tapped his forehead with a podgy forefinger.

'Come, come, Mr Perkins, now let's not be uncharitable.'

'What d'you mean, touchin' your 'ead like that,' I yelled, boiling up inside. 'I'm not daft.'

For two pins I'd have butted Mr Perkins in his fat belly – not that I was a violent sort of boy, really, just that the Perkinses of this world were a continual source of niggling, petty, adult irritation to me. Before I had decided whether such action could be justified on Holy Ground, the vicar nipped in.

[66]

'Take him to Miss Phelps and ask her to enrol him in her class. After all, if he joins us today, he'll qualify for the Sunday School Treat next month, won't he? Now there's a surprise for you, little man.'

I went red all over, specially my neck and cheeks. I turned away from Perkins because he'd be sure to read the guilt that was burning all over my face. Why else would I have trekked all this way on a Sunday morning, all dolled up in my best bib and tucker, if I hadn't known that it was St Peter's Sunday School Treat on August the fourteenth and that you had to be a member for at least a month to qualify and today was July the eleventh? And that this year they were having a special train to Marlborough Forest and there was going to be ice-cream for tea as well as corned beef sandwiches and iced buns. And that there would be games and races and competitions with real prizes for the winners (not Bibles or Hymn Books or *Lives of the Saints* like you got down at the Mission). And at the end of the day, during the train ride home, there would be an apple, an orange and a bar of chocolate for everyone.

All this and more I had heard from the lips of Ronnie Coxhead, whose Mum 'lived and died at the church' according to our Gran. She certainly did spend a lot of time at the church – besides Sundays – and what Ronnie had told me was sure to be absolute gospel truth. He had only let on because he owed me about fifty fag-cards from a playground session of 'flicks the farthest' and he couldn't meet the deadline. So he told me about the Sunday School Treat so that I could get in on it but he made me swear, 'finger wet, finger dry', that I wouldn't split the news to any of the other kids I knocked around with. It seemed a fair enough way of settling a debt – the chance of a free Sunday School Outing in lieu of fifty fag cards.

[67]

I was still blushing fiery red when the vicar spoke again, his voice coming to me as if from a long way off.

'That's surprised our little man, eh, Mr Perkins? Properly knocked him sideways, hearing about the Sunday School Treat. Gone quite pink with embarrassment, hasn't he? Sensitive little chappie, I shouldn't wonder!'

Mr Perkins uttered an almighty snort that threatened to lift the roof off the church hall. Without further words, he grabbed me by the shoulder and propelled me at arm's length into the main hall, more like a gaoler taking a criminal to clink than a Sunday School Superintendent welcoming a fresh lamb to the fold.

'Miss Phelps,' he boomed, shoving open a door at the further end of the hall. 'This one's yours. And remember – he only goes on the Treat if he turns up reg'lar and punctual the next four Sundays and his behaviour is totally impeccable. Understood? Right!'

With that, he tweaked my left ear till I thought it was going to come off in his hand, then shoved me across towards the table where a timid Miss Phelps cowered, terrified, between the two great buns of hair at either side of her face. I think she was far more scared of Mr Perkins than I was. It was some little time before she regained sufficient composure to welcome me to her class.

'We're very pleased to have you join us – er – what is your name, dear? Yes, well, never mind, dear. I never can remember little boys' names. I'll just know you're the one with the red face and the – um – unusual haircut! Find a seat, then. Over there by – um – what's-his-name – the ginger one without the front teeth.'

Thus was I enrolled into St Peter's Sunday School.

And thus was I entitled to a place on the Sunday School Treat.

Old Perkins needn't have worried. There was not the slightest danger of me missing Sunday School for the next four weeks. I would be both regular and punctual. I'd even have gone on Saturday evening and slept in the church hall all night if there had been any risk of being late on Sunday morning. Oh no, nothing could possibly happen that would prejudice my first ever chance to go on a full day Sunday School Treat – especially one that included a train ride! No! *Two* train rides. There and back again!

I had been on a few soppy, so-called Treats – things like a bun-fight in the Church Hall or a crummy concert by the Mothers' Union or some such sickening organisation – but nothing like a St Peter's Treat. They were well known to all the kids in the town. Even before Ronnie Coxhead had filled me in on the details (such as the minimum number of attendances necessary to qualify!) the fame of St Peter's Treats had spread around the backways and recreation grounds and school playgrounds for miles around. There wasn't another chapel or church that could boast a Treat anywhere near the same class as St Peter's.

As the great day approached, I began to get fits of the collywobbles like I had never had in my life before. Worrying about something dreadful happening that would prevent me going. I gave up going swimming in case I caught pneumonia – I stopped roller skating in case I broke a leg – I even packed up drinking fizzy lemonade in case it gave me stomach gripes like my Gran reckoned it gave her. I would have wrapped myself in cotton wool if I could have found a piece big enough.

'I dunno what's 'appened to you,' moaned Albie one afternoon when I turned down a ride on his Dad's old bike. 'I never 'eard you go on like this before jus' 'cos it ain't got no brakes an' one o' the pedals is missin'. I c'n remember when you come down Victoria Hill on it, scuffin' your feet on the ground so's not to 'it nothin' where it joined the main road.'

I mumbled some sort of excuse – but Albie was not satisfied.

'I can't understand it,' he went on. 'All that fuss 'cos I tapped your ankle playin' football – wastin' all the play-time standin' in a sink full o' cold water to bring out the bruise. You never used to be like it. You never used to be a – a – a cissy!'

He blurted out the word and dodged quickly away to avoid the expected thump round the ear. But I didn't react.

'There you are,' he scoffed, standing at a safe distance in case I changed my mind. 'Fancy bein' called a cissy an' not doin' nothing about it.'

It seemed to me the time had come for explanations.

'I don't wanna get 'urt, y'see, Albie, that's all it is. I jus' don't wanna miss the Treat.'

'The Treat!' Albie's big, dark eyes grew even larger. 'You don't mean – not St Peter's – ?'

I nodded.

The enormous eyes flooded with tears. 'An' you never told me,' he wept. 'You went an' joined an' you never told me why you was goin'.' His eyes sparkled through the tears as he recalled a certain Sunday. 'I remember the day. It was three Sundays ago an' you went off all dressed up an' never told me why you was goin'. Crikey! I got better friends 'n you in the zoo!'

I was quite overwhelmed. Sorry for Albie – without doubt my best mate – and angry with myself for treating him so badly.

'I'm sorry, Albie,' I said. Which was a great come-down in itself, because we hardly ever said sorry at that age. 'I couldn't tell you before 'cos Ronnie Coxhead made me promise – finger wet, finger dry, cross me 'eart an' 'ope to die – as I wouldn't split to nobody.'

'But I'm not nobody! I'm Albie. We tells each other everythin'.'

'Ronnie only told me to pay me back for some fag cards 'e owed me. Goin' on the Treat is in place o' fifty Radio Celebrities an' Hints on Association Football.'

'I'd 'ave give you an 'undred fag cards if you'd told me. I ain't never been on a Treat. Not a proper one.' His eyes overflowed again. 'I ain't never been up Marlborough Forest. An' I never been on a train ride, neither.'

I could hardly believe my ears. Never been on a train? Twelve years old and never known the thrill of jumping into a railway coach, the hiss of steam and the smell of smoke, the clackety-clack of the wheels in motion, the gently moving fields and the whizzing telegraph poles? I gazed upon Albie with deep sympathy, suddenly remembering that Albie's Dad didn't work in the railway factory like all the rest of the Dads in our street. He was about the only one who didn't. Poor old Albie. Fancy being lumbered with a Dad as didn't work on the railway. No free passes! No privilege tickets! No train rides!

'Don't worry, Albie,' I comforted him, turning my back so as not to embarrass him by letting him know I'd seen his tears. 'You can come on the Treat. I'll fix it.'

'Will you?' breathed Albie. 'Will you, really?'

Now what had I gone and done? Trust me to promise the impossible. Somebody only had to start the sob stuff and Joe Muggins would promise anything. It had been job enough getting myself admitted to the St Peter's flock right on the very stroke of the four-week-deadline to ensure qualification for the Treat. How on earth was I supposed to work a miracle and get Albie included with just four days to go?

[71]

"Ow long is it on the train to Marlborough Forest?'
asked Albie, dry-eyed and glowing. 'Is it a special jus'
for The Treat? What time do we 'ave to be at the
station? Do they really give ev'rybody a bag o' toffees
an' a banana an' a iced bun an' fish-paste sandwiches an'
a bottle of Corona an' – an' – an' ev'rythin'?'

I lay awake for ages trying to fathom out some way
of working the trick. Perhaps if I said Albie was a
patient from the Children's Hospital who had been
seriously injured in a roller-skating accident and his
doctor had begged me to arrange a sort of convalescent
day out for him? No, they'd never wear that. And
anyway, he wouldn't be able to join in all the sky-
larking if he was supposed to be that sick.

Or perhaps I could say he was my cousin who had
just been orphaned in a bush fire in Australia and only
arrived in England yesterday and I had to bring him
with me because my mother and father had gone to
Australia to see about . . . But it was getting much too
complicated that way.

It was one of those sticky August nights and I kicked
the bed-clothes on to the floor. My head was spinning
with half-baked ideas for getting Albie's name on the
list.

1 Bribery: I would pay Mr Perkins sixpence a week
for the next year if he'd slip in an extra name (I'd start
worrying about where the tanner was coming from
after the deal was done).

2 Cunning: Albie would wait on the Up Platform
while we were embarking on the Down Platform and
then he'd run across the tracks just as the train blew its
whistle and I'd open a carriage door and hoist him
aboard. (But would they know he wasn't one of us
when they started handing out the goodies?)

3 Deeper Cunning: I would find some kid who

couldn't go because he was ill (if necessary I could always poison somebody, just slightly, with a chocolate cream injected with something I'd pinch from the chem. lab at school) and then pass Albie off as the missing kid. (But one of the teachers would cotton on when they called the roll, wouldn't they?)

My mind was boiling over with plans which started off sounding perfectly reasonable and gradually became ridiculous the more I thought about them. I was hot and clammy outside – my pyjama trousers stuck to my legs like cylindrical wrappings of wet tissue paper – and all of a tizzy inside.

And then, quite suddenly, like a flash of lightning across my addled brain, I knew that there was only one way out of this maze. The usual way, of course. I would have to be very noble (the tears were already surging up), and brave (but the tears were overflowing, out of control). I would have to tell only a white lie – the sort that brought good to other people – and all would be well. For Albie. My mate.

Greater love hath no boy than he give up the Treat for his friend.

On the Friday evening before the great day I limped up the front path of Mr Perkins's private residence, my left knee swathed in half-a-mile of white, white bandage which I had found in one of the little drawers in my mother's dressing table.

I rang the bell in the centre of the front door which had stained-glass panels. Even at home Mr Perkins lived in a church!

A tall, bony woman wearing huge, horn-rimmed spectacles that covered half her face, opened the door. If she was Mrs Perkins – as indeed she turned out to be – then it looked as though her old man was eating all the food in the house and starving her to death.

'Can't you read?' she boomed in a voice too big for her body, pointing to the white enamel disc above the bell-push.

I read the cryptic message: NO HAWKERS, NO CAN-VASSERS, NO CIRCULARS.

Mrs Perkins was closing the door.

'I ain't none o' them,' I assured her. 'I ain't an 'awker nor a canvasser nor a circular!'

'What are you, then?' she demanded pompously.

'I'm a boy!' I said. And added quickly before the door could be slammed shut. 'I'm one o' Mr Perkins's boys!'

The door flew open.

'You're what?' she exploded.

'One o' Mr Perkins's Sunday School.'

'Oh! I see.' She seemed to have recovered from a shock of some sort. 'One of them – er – those.'

'Can I see Mr Perkins?'

'I don't know. Is it important?'

'Very,' I sighed, leaning heavily against the porch wall and thrusting out a stiff, bandaged leg.

'Oh! my goodness. You poor child,' clucked Mrs Perkins, coming over all motherly. 'Come on in. Here, hold my arm. No, don't put your hand all over the wallpaper.'

I limped heavily along the carpeted passage and into the room at the end. I don't know whether people like the Perkinses called it a sitting-room, dining-room, lounge or what. It was bigger than our sitting-room at home but it contained all the same sort of furniture and stuff except that theirs didn't look as though it was ever used. Like my Aunt Jessie's. They didn't have any kids either.

'There we are, then. Now you sit there and rest a minute.' She propped me in a large armchair with a pile of cushions and rested my gammy leg on a low wooden stool. 'I'll just fetch Mr Perkins from the conservatory. He's watering his pots.'

Having not the foggiest idea what a conservatory might be when it's at home and even less idea why Mr Perkins should be watering pots, I simply smiled bravely and leaned back into the cushions.

Mr Perkins arrived shortly, his quizzical gaze giving place to a kind of agonised frown when he saw who his visitor was.

'Oh! It's you, is it,' he said in his most unfriendly bellow, like the morning we first met. 'And what trouble can we expect now?'

'Arthur!' scolded Mrs Perkins. 'Can't you see the poor child has had an accident?'

Mr Perkins took in the bandages but appeared totally unimpressed. Before he could make any sarcastic retort, I nipped in.

'Mr Perkins,' I said. 'I'm afraid I won't be able to go on the Treat.'

It took the wind out of him as surely as if I'd biffed him a fourpenny one in his big, fat corporation.

'What a shame!' crooned Mrs Perkins. 'You must have been looking forward to it for so long.'

'Just a month,' leered Mr Perkins 'Ah well, there's always next year. If you keep up your attendance, that is!'

'Arthur, don't be so heartless,' Mrs Perkins chided him. 'Can't you see how upset he is.'

And indeed, I was upset, having suddenly remembered why I was here and what I was giving up.

'Arthur, go and get the chocolate biscuits.'

Mr Perkins opened his mouth to complain, then meekly trotted off to the kitchen.

'And now let me do that leg up properly,' said Mrs Perkins, sitting on the stool and resting my leg across her lap. 'Who on earth did you up like that?'

Actually, I thought I'd done a pretty good job. Well, I mean, it isn't all that easy, bandaging your own leg. But when I looked down and realised it had slipped down an inch or two already and might soon slither right down to my shoe, it didn't seem quite so good.

'Ackchully, it's not s'posed to be touched,' I informed her, giving an agonised scowl as her hand touched my leg. 'That's what they said at the 'ospital. Not to touch it until I goes up again nex' month!'

'Next month!' screeched Mrs Perkins 'I don't believe it. I'll write to the authorities about this. Which hospital? Who did you see? I'm a trained nurse, I am, and I never saw a bandage put on like that in my life, not even by a novice.'

'What's a novice?' I asked, but didn't wait for an answer as she began to unroll the yards of bandage with a very expert touch. 'Don't do that, I'll get blood pois'nin' an' gangrene an' – an' – an' things,' I ended limply as she exposed my very healthy-looking leg.

She stared unbelieving. She lifted her head and looked at me. I dropped my eyes.

'Blimey!' I said. 'It's 'ealed up already.'

Mrs Perkins bent her head low towards me. I drew away, expecting her to bawl me out. Instead, she gave me a quizzical look and whispered, 'What's the game, then, young man? Just what are you up to?'

I met her look, noticed the faintest touch of a smile on her lips and in the blue eyes behind the huge, horn-rimmed spectacles, and decided to take a chance.

'It's me mate, Albie, Mrs Perkins. It's for 'im that I done it. 'E ain't never been on a Treat. 'E ain't even been on a train.'

Mr Perkins appeared bearing the biscuit tin.

'Arthur, go and put the kettle on,' said Mrs Perkins without taking her eyes off me.

'But, Gladys – ' Mr Perkins complained.

'Now!' said Gladys.

Mr Perkins retreated to the kitchen.

'What, exactly, are you trying to say?' she demanded as soon as he had departed.

'I told you, di'n't I, it's Albie. 'E ain't never been on a Treat so I thought if I couldn't go I could put 'is name down in my place.'

'And how many Treats have you been on?' Mrs Perkins enquired gently.

''Undreds,' I lied.

'How many?'

'Well, I ain't ackchully been with your lot before but I 'ave been with the Methodists an' the Mission an' they're 'opeless, they are. St Peter's is the best, all the kids says so, ev'rybody says so an' – an' – an' Albie ain't never been on one.'

'You mean – neither of you has ever been, don't you?' She lifted my chin with the tip of a long, bony forefinger. My lips fluttered with misery. Then she bent down and began to bandage my leg, gently but firmly, with the practised hand of an expert.

'Arthur!' she called as she finished the job off with a neat little knot. 'I think he'll be well enough to go on the Treat. But he ought to bring his little friend with him just in case. He'll probably need a helping hand to get from Marlborough station up the hill into the forest!'

Albie and me sat opposite Mrs Perkins in the train on our way home from the Treat. I offered her a section of my orange.

'Thank you, dear,' she said, examining the black finger prints on the soggy bit of fruit. 'But not just now. How's your leg?'

I looked hard at her but she kept her face as straight as a die.

'Much better, thank you,' I said, seriously. 'I think today's done it good!'

'And how's – er – your friend?'

Albie, his face smudged with fish-paste, chocolate, orange and Corona, peering over a giant multi-coloured beach ball which had been first prize in the egg and spoon race, shoved another wedge of nougat into his mouth, beamed at the entire compartment and enquired stickily, 'Do we go to Marlborough ev'ry year?'

All Night Long

We sat on our front doorstep. Just Albie and me. It was September. Season of mists and marbles. Football in the street and bonfires on the allotments. The long, light nights behind us and Christmas too far ahead to start thinking about yet.

'What's it like in ole Taffy McNab's class, Albie?'

We'd been back at school about a week. Although our birthdays were within a few weeks of each other, they fell on opposite sides of September the first, so I was a year above Albie.

''E ain't so bad as they all reckoned. 'E've only clipped me ear a couple o' times,' said Albie. ''E ain't give me the cane yet.'

'What sort o' things d'you do?' I asked, scuffing the pavement with the iron studs in the heel of my boot.

'I dunno.' Albie screwed up his eyes and pursed his lips with the effort of trying to remember. 'Nothin' much.'

'You mus' do summat,' I persisted. 'You can't sit there all day an' not do nothin'.'

'Jography,' Albie said suddenly.

'Eh?'

'Jography. That's what we done 'safternoon. Jography.'

'What sort?'

'King Alfred,' said Albie brightly.

I looked up from my scuffing, incredulous. ''E ain't jography. 'E's 'istory!' I jeered.

''Ow d'you know?' Albie shoved his hair back out of his eyes and gave me a sceptical glower.

''Cos jography's about countries,' I said loftily. There wasn't much I didn't know even when I was only twelve!

'Well, Alfred lived in a country, di'n't he?' protested Albie. 'Ev'rybody lives in a country. Alfred lived 'ere.'

'So, 'cordin' to you, then, every time you talks about anybody it mus' be jography, seein' as ev'rybody lives somewhere,' I sneered.

Albie searched for an answer.

'I ain't arguin' wi' you,' he said eventually. He never argued with me. He was better at fighting than me but his mind wasn't as nimble as his fists. 'All I'm sayin' is, we done King Alfred. You asked me what we done an' I told you.'

I didn't want a scrap with Albie and finish the day bad friends so I shut up and scuffed my initials in the dust with my heel.

''E burnt the cakes,' Albie announced after a lengthy silence.

''Oo did?'

'Alfred did. We was talkin' about Alfred, wasn't we? Well, 'e burnt the cakes.'

'Sounds more like cookery than jography,' I scoffed.

'You dunno nothin' 'bout King Alfred, you don't,' said Albie heatedly. 'You're tryin' to be funny 'cos you don't know nothin' about 'im an' you don't like it 'cos I know summat you don't know.'

'Me! Not know nothin' 'bout King Alfred!' I stalled for time, scratching around the recesses of my memory

[80]

for something about Alfred. 'Course I do! Well, I mean – er – 'e was a good king, wasn't 'e?'

Albie looked nonplussed.

''Ow do I know if 'e was any good? All I know is 'e burnt the cakes. An' I don't see 'ow 'e could 'ave been all that good if 'e couldn't stop a few cakes from burnin'.'

I was vastly intrigued by all this stuff about Alfred's lack of success with his cooking. It was news to me, though I couldn't help feeling Albie had got it wrong somewhere.

'You dunno what you're on about, Albie Cullingford. What's a king doin' makin' cakes, eh? Well, I mean – kings might 'ave been poorer in them days than what King George the Sixth is now – but they couldn't 'ave been that poor!'

'It wasn't 'is cakes,' explained Albie, very patiently, as if he was addressing an idiot. ''E was lookin' after 'em for somebody else.'

I leapt to my feet, shaking with laughter. 'The king! Goin' round 'elpin' in people's kitchens! Oh crikey, Albie, you don't 'alf get 'old o' some rubbish! I s'pose you'll be tellin' me next 'e was busy duckin' out a few nappies an' 'e forgot to turn the gas stove off!'

Albie rose slowly to his feet. He stood a full inch taller than me. When he was angry his eyes bulged like marbles and his lips were a thin line hiding his clenched teeth.

'You knows everythin', don't you, Mr Clever Dick,' he hissed in my face. 'Or you thinks you do. Well, when you goes indoors, you find your fag-card c'lection of Kings an' Queens of England an' 'ave a look on the back of Alfred. Then you'll bloomin' soon find out who knows what 'e's on about.'

And with that, Albie stomped off across the road to

his house and slammed the front door so hard behind him I wonder every window in the block didn't fall out in sympathy.

I sat on, alone, as the September night gathered itself around me, expecting any second to hear my mother shriek for me to, 'Come in an' get washed an' into bed!' I was still musing on the unlikely picture of Alfred, crown askew, clutching a tray of charred fairy cakes, when an incredible procession came into view. It was, without any doubt, the most eerie, the most nightmarish, the most unforgettable vision that my twelve-year-old eyes had yet witnessed.

In front, a man in a long black cloak over which he wore what looked like a white, lace-edged shirt, walking very slowly, carrying something in front of him. A sort of pole? As he stepped into the greenish-yellow glow of the street lamp on the corner, something flashed and sparkled, and I saw he was carrying a cross and was wearing the white and black uniform of the church.

Behind him came another man in surplice and cassock, swinging a silver pot on a chain. The inside of the pot glowed red and a sickly-sweet smoke curled out of it and lay over the narrow street like a scented mist. By his side, a tiny fair-haired boy, scarce old enough to be in the baby class at infant school, toddled along carrying a kind of silver bowl in his cupped hands.

But it was what followed next that made my heart leap inside me and the short hairs at the nape of my neck begin to crawl. The gleaming chrome and polished glass of J. J. Jones and Sons (Undertakers) brand-new Bentley hearse, with Death Driver Charlie Forbes at the wheel and old Mr J. J. Jones, in person and top-hat, sitting at his side. The pale, wooden coffin, its shiny handles like door knockers, a single bunch of flowers on top, seemed to fill the rest of the vehicle. Walking alongside the hearse, four on each side, were young men carrying tall candles which flickered and flared and lit the macabre scene by fits and starts.

I stared after the incredible procession, hardly daring to breath, totally unable to move.

I'd seen plenty of funerals before. We passed J. J. Jones and Sons (Undertakers) on our way to school. Old Charlie, the Death Driver, often threatened to box us up and take us on our last, long ride if we touched the mirror-like bonnet of his hearse with our mucky hands. I'd watched him and the lads in the workshop loading up – I could tell by the way they handled the coffin whether it was empty or engaged. Nothing about funerals in the day-time frightened me in the least (though I did often wonder how Charlie would come off if a box ever got free of its moorings and slid forward and clumped him in the back of his head!).

But a funeral at night! Death and darkness hand in hand. 'The grave as little as my bed,' we used to sing at morning assembly, and I always had terrible dreams the night after we'd sung it. If people had to die, and it seemed to be the accepted thing, then at least they ought to do it in the daylight. And be buried in the light, naturally.

Surely they wouldn't – ! No, of course not. It was the wrong way for the cemetery. But where were they going? Did they have a special burial place for night funerals? I'd read stories about digging up bodies in the dead of night – to sell for doctors to practise on or to rob them of their rings and jewels – but I'd never heard of the other way round. What did a person have to do to get buried at night?

Suddenly, I got up and ran. Drawn like a moth to the candlelight – drugged by the cloying smell of the incense – hypnotised by the rear-lights of J. J. Jones and Sons' (Undertakers) magnificent hearse – I followed on like a child who had heard the call of the Pied Piper. I had to know! If they travelled a hundred miles and it took all night to get there – I still had to know!

In fact, they travelled less than one mile. I caught up with them just before they reached the church. I stood – a small, bewildered figure – on the opposite pavement while Charlie and three assistants scooped the coffin on to their shoulders. A priest stood in the dimly-lit church porch, like St Peter at the gates of Paradise. He bowed to the advancing cortège, turned, and was followed into the vast interior by the man with the cross, the man with the incense, the men with the candles, and finally, the men with the coffin.

An unseen hand closed the doors. Like the curtains silently closing at the pictures. I wouldn't have been surprised if the words THE END had flashed up on the doors. The gaggle of silent spectators broke up and went their separate ways. But I stayed on. This was not THE END for me. It was only the first instalment of the serial and I had to find out what happened next.

After a while – ten minutes – half-an-hour? – what is time when one's thoughts are busy with the mystery of life and death? – Charlie and his three mates came out, climbed into the hearse, and purred off past the Town Hall and back towards the garage at the back of J. J. Jones and Sons (Undertakers).

Now what? Had they buried it inside the church? A sort of underground chamber like I'd seen in drawings of the pyramids? But they couldn't have had a proper service, there hadn't been any people in other cars, like at normal funerals.

I looked up at the enormous stained-glass windows and they twinkled faintly red and blue from the thin, yellow light on the inside. Were the men with the candles still there? And the one swinging the incense? Or was there a back door for the priest and the others to get out by?

Abruptly, I crossed the road, lifted the heavy, cold latch, pushed open the door, slid inside, closed it behind me – and stood there, panting, trembling, dying to know yet afraid to look.

'What you reckon you'm up to, then?'

The double shock of that unearthly voice and the hand that gripped my shoulder almost made me a candidate for my own funeral.

'After pinchin' the c'lection money, is it?'

The voice moved round until it was in front of me. It came from a big mouth full of uneven, brown teeth in a deeply-lined face topped by a tuft of spiky, grey hair. The owner must have been about six times as old as me, but not a lot taller – a dwarfish old man, obviously the doorkeeper. (If churches have doorkeepers?) I couldn't help thinking of the Hunchback of Notre Dame. I wouldn't have been surprised if he'd suddenly shinned up a rope into the belfry, carrying me with him.

'Ain't yer got a voice in yer 'ead, then,' he went on. ''Ere, I knows you –' he squinted at me thoughtfully – 'you'm the one as drunk the communion wine, ain't yer?'

'No!' I squealed. Even when caught doing something wrong, it still hurt to be accused of a crime one wouldn't dream of committing. 'I ain't never been in 'ere never before. Honest, mister!'

'Then what you doin' 'ere now, eh? Answer me that!'

I remembered what I was here for all right. But how to tell a grown-up? How to ask this wizened dwarf, who still clung to me like an avenging angel making an arrest, all the questions I needed an answer to? And anyway – where was it?

'I come to see what's 'appenin',' I said limply.

'Oh! Did we now! An' what did we expect to find – besides the c'lection money – Arsenal versus Aston Villa?'

'No, no,' I protested. 'I come to see what's 'appened to the – the – the coffin!'

My voice broke on the dreadful word. The grip on my shoulder loosened. The old man peered even more closely into my face.

'You related?' he enquired gently.

'Eh?'

'To the deceased?' He jerked his head violently to the left.

I followed the direction of the jerk. A long way off – up towards the towering, stained-glass windows, in front of the altar, and between the inward-facing seats where I knew the choirboys sat, was a purple and gold cloth which appeared to be suspended in mid-air about six feet off the ground. It hung there, like a rich table-cloth, and at each corner of the table stood one of the candle-bearing men, head bowed, facing outwards. Obviously on guard. And I knew what they were guarding, what was hidden under the table-cloth.

I took an involuntary step forward.

'Don't go up there.' The voice took on a new quality – understanding, sympathetic. 'Is 'e – I mean, was 'e – yer Gramp?'

'No. 'E ain't – I mean, wasn't – me Gramp. I dunno 'oo 'e was. I jus' – well, wanted to know what was 'appenin' to 'im.'

He grabbed me again, as if to chuck me out. I'd been chucked out of enough places to recognise the signs.

'I ain't doin' no 'arm,' I pleaded. 'I followed 'em all the way 'ere an' I jus' came in to see why.'

'Why what?'

'Why 'e come tonight. I mean, I never seen nobody buried at night.'

'Well, now you know, then. 'E ain't buried. 'E'm jus' lyin' in.'

'Lyin' in? What for?'

''Cos that's what 'e asked for when 'e 'ad the last rites. 'E was a big worker in the church an' that's what 'e wanted.'

'What's last rites?'

'You wants to know a lot in an 'urry, don't yer?'

I gazed transfixed at the tableau near the altar.

'What 'appens next?' I asked.

'Requiem mass, nine o'clock.'

'Is 'e goin' to stay there all night, then?'

'Well, 'e ain't likely to get up an' go nowhere, is 'e?'

The old chap gave a wheezy chuckle. I glared at him. I could have hit him, saying a thing like that at a time like this. A fine, holy doorkeeper he was. I thought about reporting him to the vicar.

'My Gramp done 'is lyin' in in our front room,' I said.

'Yeah, well, most people do, I s'pose. But if you'm cath'lic, you can lie in church the night afore,' my tutor explained.

'Does it 'elp? I mean, does it make 'im better than our Gramp if 'e stays 'ere all night an' 'as a mast at nine o'clock?'

'I don't s'pose so,' he said – and added, after some consideration – 'Depends what you b'lieves in, I reckon.'

'I b'lieves in lyin' in in our front room an' bein' buried prop'ly in the day-time an' goin' to 'eaven,' I announced firmly.

'Mm, well, I s'pect it's all diff'rent routes to the same place.' He nodded gravely. ''Cept that the cath'lics knows the best an' quickest way!'

He grinned, displaying all his rotten teeth. I thought a

toothbrush and half-a-pound of soot would have done him more good than his cath'lic religion.

'Oo are you, then?' I asked finally, dragging my gaze away from the main attraction.

'Me!' He wound himself up to a full five feet. 'Me! I'm the verger, I am.'

'What's a – ?' I began, but he was already shoving me out of the door.

'You've asked enough questions for one night. Gerroff 'ome an' say a prayer for the repose o' the soul o' the departed.'

'Repose o' what?'

But the door had closed behind me and I was back in the world of the living. Mind you, as I started to walk home, living and dying seemed much closer together than they had earlier in the evening.

Suddenly, I turned and rushed back to the church. Hunchback barred my way before I'd half opened the door.

'What about them?' I gasped, pointing.

'Them?' He hesitated in the act of chucking me out. 'Them who?'

'The candle men,' I said. 'They got to stand there all night, without movin', till the nine o'clock mast?'

'Mass,' he corrected me. 'Requiem mass. An' the answer is no – they changes ev'ry two hours.'

'Could I – well, you know – could I stay an' see 'em change over?'

I thought for a moment he was going to land me one on the jaw. On sacred ground! Well, only just outside sacred ground, anyway!

I got into the biggest row for ages when I finally got home. My mother had scoured the streets, my father had searched the rec, and they reckoned they were going to have the canal dragged, when I eventually walked in. But even a couple of thumps round the ear and getting sent to bed with no supper and a certain promise that I wouldn't be getting my Friday penny, couldn't switch off the pictures in my mind – the ghostly procession, the candles, the incense, the gleaming hearse, the purple cloth beneath the tall windows. In a way, I wished my two clips on the ear had been strong enough to empty my head of all that I had seen and heard and smelled that night. Then, perhaps, there wouldn't be the inevitable nightmares . . .

'What 'appened to you las' night?' Albie greeted me when I called for him the next morning.

'Nothin' much,' I said, carelessly.

'I 'eard your Mam yellin' out for you to come in for ages. She di'n't 'alf sound mad.'

'I wasn't all that late. I dunno what she makes such a fuss about. 'Alf 'er life she spends tellin' me to get out from under 'er feet an' the other 'alf carryin' on somethin' alarmin' 'cos I've done what she asked!' I kicked up a bit of loose paving stone and side-footed it expertly across to Albie. 'Anyway,' I said, truthfully, 'I went to church.'

Albie laughed so much he made a shocking mess of passing the stone back to me and I had to fetch it from the other side of the road.

'What for?' he spluttered between great gusts of laughter. 'To 'ave a sup at the communion wine?'

Why did everyone think I was addicted to communion wine? I mean to say, just because my Dad liked a couple o' pints didn't meant I was alcoholic.

'It was to do with lyin' in an' requiem mast an' reposin' souls,' I said loftily.

But Albie just looked at me dead blank.

When we arrived at J.J. Jones and Sons (Undertakers), old Charlie was there, as usual, polishing away at his pride and joy as if he was trying to rub a hole in the gleaming bonnet.

'Keep yer mucky 'ands off 'er,' he admonished us while we were still ten yards away.

'I seen you las' night,' I said to him, very confidential like. 'I seen the procession.'

'Oh aye!' said Charlie, still polishing. 'What d'you think of it then? Better than the town carnival?'

He began to laugh and his reflection laughed back at him from the burnished metal of the hearse. Why did everyone find it so funny when it was really such a serious, mystifying business?

'They'll be doin' the requiem mast soon,' I said.

'Oh aye, so they will.' Charlie took his silver watch out of his waistcoat pocket. ''Ave to be off soon an' c'lect 'im.'

'C'lect 'im?'

'Can't leave 'im clutterin' up the church, can we now? 'E've got the last lap still to do.'

And with that Charlie folded his duster and disappeared into the yard.

'What's all that about, then?' asked Albie.

'Oh, nothin',' I said casually. 'Jus' summat I found out about las' night.'

'D'you find out about Alfred?' Albie stuck his elbow in my ribs. 'I bet you di'n't. I bet you was afraid to look 'im up in case I was right.'

'Albie!' I caught him by the sleeve of his jersey. 'Was Alfred a cath'lic?'

'A cath'lic what?'

'You know – cath'lic religion.'

Albie pondered. 'I dunno,' he said. 'Taffy never said nothin' 'bout 'im goin' to church. Tell you what, tho',' he added brightly, 'our Auntie Phyllis is. She married one, so now our Mam says she's one 'erself!'

[90]

'Can anybody be one?' I asked.

But Albie had lost interest in the subject and was doing a bit of fancy footwork with a stone in the gutter. At the school gate he turned to me and demanded brusquely, 'You ain't goin' to change from bein' a Christian?'

'I dunno, Albie. But I might 'ave to.' The five to nine bell began to toll. 'Y'see, I been thinkin'. It's bound to be better to do your lyin' in in church than in our front room at 'ome. Don't you reckon?' Albie gazed at me, his brow furrowed with the effort of trying to comprehend. And the heavy, black, school bell clanged mournfully on. 'Y'see, Albie, if you're goin' to 'eaven it seems more proper to be in church the las' night you're 'ere, 'cos it's sort of 'alf-way there. An' our front room's terrible damp an' we gets mice in there sometimes an' our Gran keeps 'er bottles o' stout be'ind the sofa.' The bell stopped, half-way through a clang. We belted for the door.

"Albie,' I whispered as we entered the long corridor which was an area of UTTER SILENCE, 'I'd rather 'ave four candle men on guard an' a verger on the door than be left on me own, wouldn't you?'

The Final Demand

'We've 'ad our 'lectric cut off,' Albie announced proudly.

'You 'ad what?' I stopped in the middle of sorting out my fag cards of Radio Celebrities, Stainless Stephen in one hand and Charlie Kunz in the other.

'You don't never listen to what I say firs' time,' Albie complained sadly. 'You wanna get your ear'oles cleaned out.'

He obviously wanted to impress me. He was sitting, cross-legged, on our coal-bunk, looking a bit like an undersized Indian beggar with his dark, floppy hair and black eyes set deep in his sun-tanned face.

I was impressed, too. It was something that had never happened in our house. We'd had the yard dug up and half the floor-boards in the kitchen when we had a gas leak, but we'd never had the electric cut off.

'I did 'ear,' I said, trying to sound casual. 'But I didn't know 'xac'ly 'ow you meant "cut off".'

'Well, 'ow many ways can you cut it off?' Albie asked sarcastically.

'With a knife? Or a pair o' scissors?' I had all sorts of bright ideas flashing through my head. 'Or –?'

'Stop muckin' about,' Albie interrupted. 'You're only jealous 'cos you've never 'ad it done.'

''Ow d'you know we 'aven't?'

''Cos you'd 'ave never stopped goin' on about it if you 'ad,' Albie stated with some truth.

'What d'you 'ave it cut off for?' I asked – as if I didn't know. And to give Albie his moment of glory.

''Cos we 'adn't paid our bill!'

He nearly rolled off the coal-bunk he was so puffed up with pride.

He would have to be the one who had an exciting tale like that to boast about. We'd been a bit near it in our house once or twice – I could remember my Mam running all the way down to the Less Giggity Office (a name which I gave the local Electricity department at the age of two and which remained an unfunny, embarrassing joke in our family forever after) in order to beat the deadline of the final Final Demand.

But I'd never actually been lucky enough to see the men in their peak caps and navy blue raincoats come and turn it off.

''Ow did they do it?' I asked grudgingly.

'What d'you mean, 'ow d'they do it?'

'Jus' what I say. 'Ow do they cut it off?'

I had to know. I'd have even given him my Stuart Hibberd to hear all the sordid details.

Albie pierced me with those deep, dark eyes. I thought for a dreadful moment he wasn't going to tell – that he wouldn't share the experience – not even with me, his best mate.

Then he said, meekly, 'I dunno. They went in the pantry, where our meter is, an' when they come out, it was done.'

'What!' I said aghast. 'Di'n't they dig nothin' up?'

Albie shook his head. 'There's nothin' in it! Nothin' to watch. I can't even see 'ow they done it – I looked an' looked in our pantry but all the wires is still there. An' the meter!'

I suddenly lost all interest in having one's electricity cut off. If there wasn't anything to see – no workmen digging up the garden or the front pavement – no carting off of meters and sundry appliances in full view of the neighbours – then it wasn't worth getting a bad name up and down the street.

'The best bit was last night,' Albie chirped up quickly. 'Our Aunt Nancy came round an' when it started to get dark they tried to get 'er to go 'ome but she kept on stoppin' an' in the end they could 'ardly see one another 'cross the room an' our Dad said 'e was sorry there wasn't no light 'cos we'd blown a fuse! An' our Aunt Nancy said if 'e di'n't know 'ow to mend a fuse she'd show 'im an' 'e got all nasty an' they finished off 'avin' a lovely row all in the dark!'

I went on sorting my fag cards while Albie continued to squat on the bunk, still cock-a-hoop because his family were poorer, and more susceptible and long-suffering than mine.

'Tell you what,' I said, the subject of electricity completely erased from my mind. 'I'll give you Jack Payne, Anona Winn an' the Western Brothers for Ambrose. C'mon, Albie, I only needs three for the set.'

'We only wants another five bob,' Albie muttered.

'Well, I like that!' I exploded. 'You got the cheek to go on at me for not listenin' proper. What you talkin' about five bobs for?'

'That's all we wants. To pay the 'lectric.'

'You mean if your Mam 'ad another five bob you could get it cut on again?'

'Yeah,' said Albie, drilling compassionate holes in me with those big eyes.

And so – the idea of having one's electricity supply cut off having lost its appeal – what did seem important was that a matter of a few shillings could restore Albie's power supply and, presumably, their family pride. Although Albie saw the actual cutting off as a notable event in his life and one not experienced by any of his mates down the street – not yet, at any rate – it was obvious that there were plenty of reasons why he would now want it on again. For his Mam's sake. (Although she was fat and floppy and had lumpy, purple legs, Albie seemed to like her.) And because of the dark. I was probably the only person in the whole of Albie's world who knew his dreadful secret. He was scared sick of going to bed in the dark.

'It's a lot o' money,' I said, having given the matter considerable thought.

'I know,' Albie murmured. 'Me Dad says if 'e changed from Gold Flake to Woodbines 'e could save fourpence a day. 'Ow long would that take to make five bob?'

Albie had great faith in my mental arithmetic.

In due course I gave him his answer.

'More 'n a fortnight.'

'Crikey!' was all he could say.

I don't know why I say these daft things on impulse but it seemed there was only one thing that could be said. So I said it. 'We'll get the money, Albie.'

'Eh?'

'We'll get it. Today.'

Why I had to go and say today I just don't know! But there it was – said. And Albie scrambling down off our coal-bunk, his skimpy grey trousers all covered in coal dust and his face shining with gratitude. He had real faith in me, Albie did.

'How?' he enquired gently.

'Well – er – you know, I'll think o' summat.'

The light in his eyes went out as if his own personal electric supply had been disconnected.

'What I mean is,' I corrected myself quickly, 'I know what we're goin' to do. It's jus' figurin' out the details needs thinkin' about.'

Albie's light was switched on again.

'If you only needs five bob,' I said, 'why don't your Dad jus' sell summat? Like the front-room sofa – or the wireless – or your Mam's best coat?'

I was a logical little devil even at that age.

'Because,' Albie replied, equally logically, 'the sofa's got bits o' spring an' stuffin' stickin' out – the wireless ain't ours, we rents it – an' our Mam only got one coat an' I don't reckon Scraggy 'Arry, the rag an' bone man, would give 'er nothin' for it neither!'

'You mean you ain't got nothin' in your 'ouse worth five measly bob?'

'All the stuff in our 'ouse put together wouldn't 'ardly be worth five bob! An' anyway,' Albie added, 'me Dad says once you gets rid of things, you never seems to be able to get enough money together to ever get 'em back again.'

'OK.' I put a hand on Albie's shoulder in the special sort of way we seemed to do when one of our tribe needed help. 'We'll get it all right. Don't you worry. We'll get it.'

By twelve o'clock we had twopence ha'penny.

We had been earning at the rate of about a penny an hour and we had exhausted every possible avenue.

Albie's Uncle Bob gave us a penny for shifting a pile of bricks from one end of his yard to the other. About a million bricks judging from the pain in my thin arms. And only a penny between us. Not even one each!

Then we walked about a mile to my Uncle Charlie's but there was nobody home. My Uncle George would have been good for a copper or two but he was in hospital with his ulcer and I knew my Auntie Doll had

[96]

no pennies to spare. In desperation I tried my own domicile.

'Get off with you,' my Mum said. 'You 'ad your Friday penny yesterday. You think I'm made o' money, you do!'

'Shove off!' my Dad said. 'No! 'Ang on a tick. Ol' Percy Thompson said 'e 'ad a hundredweight o' slack coal 'e'd give us to burn in the copper. You can find a wheelbarrow an' go an' shovel it out of 'is coal'ouse if you like.'

An hour later there was a wheelbarrow load of slack in our coal bunk, me and Albie looked more like the Kentucky Minstrels than normal – and we had acquired a second penny.

Considering how we slaved for those two pennies it seemed positively unfair that Albie got the odd ha'penny simply by thumping the Beechnut chewing gum machine outside the corner shop!

Normally we'd have put the ha'penny back in the machine (every fourth coin you got two packets for the price of one!), but today we needed every miserable ha'penny we could scrape up.

'We ain't gonna do it, are we?' Albie looked up from his chips, but I avoided his gaze. I busied myself with my own dinner. We sat on Albie's garden wall, a *Daily Herald* full of chips between us, sludged with salt, soaked in vinegar and, when we picked them up in our fingers, spiced with coal dust.

We had intended to forego our Saturday dinner and put an extra tuppence in the kitty but once we had our chip money in our grubby fists and the aroma of Bulgarelli's fish and chip shop in our nostrils, we just had to eat.

'We'll do better 'safternoon,' I cheered Albie. 'When we've got some grub inside us.'

'I weren't 'alf 'ungry,' Albie slobbered through a mouthful of half-chewed chips. 'All them bricks! An' that coal! It's the 'ardest Saturday mornin' I ever 'ad. I think I'd rather 'ave been at school!'

Well, I thought, there's gratitude for you. I'd worked every bit as hard as him and it wasn't doing me a scrap of good. It was his lousy electric bill we were trying to pay.

As if reading my thoughts, Albie said, 'You'll think of summat after we've ate these. You always do.'

I felt better for that. I took a great fistful of chips and blew on them. One thing about old Bulgarelli's chips – they were always hot enough to set your teeth on edge.

'If we don't get it switched on today,' Albie piped up out of the blue, 'I'm gonna miss the Ovaltineys tomorrow afternoon.'

I could recognise a personal tragedy when I met one.

'That's all right,' I comforted him. 'You can come over our 'ouse an' 'ear it. As long as you don't put your feet up on the furniture like you did las' time,' I added pointedly, recalling that Albie was currently suspended from entering our place because of his careless habits with his footwear.

Our fingers met in the centre of the crumpled newspaper as we battled for the last handful of chips.

'What we gonna do, then?' Albie licked the salt and vinegar residue off his fingers and wiped them on his jersey.

'I can't tell you till I've ate these chips,' I lied, my mind whirling with ideas, some daft and some even dafter. 'You're not s'posed to talk while you're eatin'!'

I chomped away slowly, like a small cow chewing its cud, waiting for the light to dawn.

It did. Quite suddenly.

'Ready, then?' I said, tossing the soggy remains of the

Daily Herald into Mrs Pebworthy's garden and leaping off the wall as if I'd known all along where we were going next.

'Where to?' asked Albie.

'The 'elpin' 'and.'

'The 'oo?'

'The 'elpin' 'and.'

'Where's that?'

'Town 'all. The Mayor's 'elpin' 'and fund.'

'What Mayor?'

'What d'you mean, what Mayor? There's only one Mayor! The chief man at the Town 'all. The 'ead one.'

'Oh!' said Albie.

When my Uncle Bill was on the dole I heard him telling Mam how the Helping Hand Fund had dubbed up some cash to help him pay his rent, and they sometimes helped my Auntie Doll whenever Uncle George's ulcer put him back in hospital and she had nothing to feed Joan, Doreen, Daph and baby Arthur on by the end of the week. (And I know that's true because I've been to their house and actually seen little Arthur in his high chair gnawing on the last crust of bread in the house while the others sat round and watched him.)

'Gerrout!' bellowed the bloke on guard in the Town Hall, the second me and Albie poked our noses round the door.

'You dunno what we come for yet,' I countered, not to be put off. ''Ow d'you know it ain't nothin' important?'

''Cos I seen enough o' your sort before.' He made a move towards the door. 'An' your sort spells trouble with a capital T!'

'I wanna see the Mayor,' I demanded.

'Oh aye! I s'pose you got an appointment?'

'Well, no, not 'xactly. I didn't know nothin' 'bout 'pointments. I jus' wants to see 'im.'

''E ain't 'ere,' said the janitor, easing us back towards the door. ''E don't work Saturdays. An' even if 'e did, 'e wouldn't want to see the likes o' you!'

'Oh yes, 'e would!' I said defiantly. 'Ol' Mr Sharpe at school said the Mayor was 'ead man in the town an' 'e made sure we was ruled over proper an' we was all treated fair. I come to see 'im 'bout 'is 'elpin' 'and fund.'

'I'll give you an 'elpin' 'and round yer ear if you don't get off that tiled floor. I jus' scrubbed that lot, I 'ave.'

Albie and I sat on the Town Hall steps.

'Bloomin' 'eck!' I swore vividly. 'Fancy 'avin' an 'elpin' 'and fund that don't 'elp on Sat'days! An' fancy allowin' people like 'im to treat citizens like you an' me the way 'e did. If only it was in the old days we could get Robin 'ood on to 'im! Or get Guy Fawkes to blow 'im up! Ennit always the way? Years an' years you an' me 'aven't asked for nothin' an' the first time we needs 'elp it 'appens to be on a Sat'day an' they don't 'elp nobody Sat'days. I reckon that's loonie, that is. 'Ow you s'posed to arrange it, so's you don't need 'elp Sat'days, that's what I'd like to know!'

'Shurrup gon' on an' on,' said Albie. 'It won't change nothin', you jus' keepin' on an' on like that.'

'Well! I like that!' I stood up. ''Ere I'm wastin' my Sat'day on your ol' 'lectric bill an' all you can say is I'm goin' on an' on. If you think that was goin' on an' on you wants to 'ear me when I'm reely goin' on an' on!'

'Why don't we go an' watch the cricket?' Albie said.

'Eh?'

'The GWR first eleven are playin' Chelt'n'am. They're a good team. My Dad says they're a lot o' toffee-nosed sods lives in Chelt'n'am but they 'as a good cricket team 'cos they're not workin' class like our team. They're gentlemen!'

[100]

'I thought we was s'posed to be tryin' to make money,' I exploded. 'Not watchin' cricket matches.'

'I thought you liked cricket,' said Albie. 'You're always captain when we picks sides an' you're Wally 'ammond when you're battin' an' Larwood when you're bowlin'.'

''Ere,' I said. 'D'you reckon ol' Fatty Arbuckle on the gate might let us 'elp 'im take the money?'

Albie shook his head.

'Or sell score cards?'

More solemn head-shaking.

'Or 'elp sellin' cups o' tea?'

A final, definite shake.

''Ow we ever gonna make that money?' I cried in desperation. 'Don't nobody trust us!'

'Don't worry,' said Albie. 'You tried real 'ard. You thought o' lots o' things. It wasn't your fault none of 'em was no good!'

I gave Albie one of my withering glances. It was wasted on him. You can't wither the Albies of this world. 'C'mon,' I said. 'If Chelt'n'am's battin' first, we'll get down by the sight screen an' see if we can get some of 'em out by jumpin' up an' down jus' as the bowler's goin' to bowl!'

We got into the cricket ground free by one of our normal methods. First, I approached Fatty Arbuckle, the gateman, and told him I'd seen some kids trying to climb the fence behind the pavilion. While I was show-ing him the place and looking mystified because there was no one there, Albie nipped through the gate and mingled with the crowd around the score-board. Then, after a suitable interval, Albie rushed up to Fatty, gesticulating wildly and yelling about kids trying to climb the fence and get in for nothing. Fatty deserted his pay-box once more to inspect the fence from the inside.

In a flash, I was through the gate and before you could say Marylebone Cricket Club me and Albie were part of the scenery, lying there on the warm, close-cropped grass, elbows an inch from the white-painted boundary line, chins cupped in hands, looking for all the world as if we had been there since the start of play.

'Crikey! What a slog!' cried Albie as the ball flew over our heads for a six.

'They might be gentlemen,' I sneered, 'but they can't bowl for toffee, this Chelt'n'am lot. Ol' Charlie Spurlock what 'it that six only works down the coal yard.'

'P'r'aps being gentlemen they bats better than they bowls,' Albie suggested.

I jerked a thumb up towards the big, square, tin numbers hanging on the scoreboard. 'They've already been in. They only made a 'undred an' twenty. We'll beat 'em easy.'

'We must 'ave missed a lot,' Albie said.

'Course we missed a lot! We was up the Town 'all, wasn't we? Seems to me the 'ole day's been a bit of a waste. Workin' like slaves an' thinkin' up things when we should've been restin' our brains ready for nex' week. An' all we've got is tuppence ha'penny.'

'Never mind,' said Albie. 'It was a good try. You can let your brain 'ave a rest now 'cos the 'lectricity place'll be shut by now so it's too late to pay it today.'

We lay, side by side, as the sun dipped into evening and the cricket match moved towards a peaceful end.

A young chap sitting near us got up to go. As he stood and stretched his cramped muscles a ten bob note fluttered from a pocket of his grey flannel trousers and settled itself against the leg of one of the wooden benches which were set at intervals around the boundary.

I looked at Albie.

[102]

Albie returned the look.

The young man was strolling away towards the exit. Another few seconds – another few yards – and he would be out of earshot.

I looked at Albie.

He was leaving the decision to me.

'Hey, mister!' I yelled. 'Hey! You've dropped summat.'

I felt greatly relieved once it was out. Quite saintly, in fact. I could feel the halo resting lightly a foot or so above my head.

The young man did not hear. I picked up the note and ran after him before any second thoughts could shatter the recently acquired halo. 'Please, mister, you dropped this.'

The young man gave me the normal sort of sidelong glance that grown-ups usually bestow on small scruffy boys who intrude on their privacy. Then he saw the crinkled, brown note in my fingers and his own hand flew to his pocket – and came out empty.

'Thanks – er – um – thanks very much,' he stammered. It was probably the first time he had ever had to say thank you to anybody like me. 'D'you fancy an ice-cream?'

By that time, Albie had joined us. He made sure there were no more beneficiaries, then added: 'Both of you?'

'I'll 'ave a raspberry an' vanilla wafer,' said Albie.

'Oh no you won't!' I chipped in. 'You're not allowed to eat ice-cream with your stomach. You know what the doctor said.' I turned to the bewildered young man. ''E don't get much proper food, see, what with 'is dad on the dole an' 'is mother bein' took away –' I tapped my forehead with my finger sadly – 'so 'is stomach ain't strong enough to 'ave ice-cream, so when any kind gen'leman offers us a reward for findin' 'is ten bob note,

[103]

we always takes the money so as we can buy food for all the rest of 'is starvin' fam'ly.'

The young man looked nonplussed. I was now well and truly airborne on my flight of fancy.

'Y'see, mister, there's six of 'em an' my friend 'ere, 'e's the eldest, and none of 'em ain't 'ad nothin' to eat since – when was it you 'ad them crisps, Wednesday or Thursday? – an' it's gonna cost a fortune for funerals if they all goes an' dies of starvation an' 'as to be –'

'Here,' the young man cut me off in mid-flow, 'take this for your cheek. And don't spend it all at once.'

He flipped a silver coin into the air. Albie lunged, I jogged his elbow with my left hand and caught the florin in my right.

'A two bob bit!' squealed Albie.

'Thanks, miser.' I remembered my manners.

'Well, I mus' say you're a great 'elp, I don't think.' I rounded on Albie, mimicking his voice. ' "I'll 'ave a raspberry an' vanilla wafer!" Jus' fancy! After all I've bin through today tryin' to get money for your rotten ol' 'lectric bill an' you goes an' says you'll 'ave an ice-cream. D'you think I don't fancy one? I'm near dyin' o' thirst ever since I put all that salt on me chips!'

'I forgot,' Albie said simply.

'You'd forget your 'ead if it wasn't screwed on.'

'I don't think much of you tellin' 'im our Mam was a bit touched,' Albie complained bitterly. 'An' all that stuff about dyin' o' starvation an' not 'avin' nothin' to eat since las' Wednesday an' all that.'

'Well, 'e coughed up two bob, di'n't 'e? Jus' a couple o' little lies brings in two bob after floggin' our guts out all mornin' for two crummy pence. Makes being honest seem like a waste of a mornin'. Anyway –' I concluded virtuously, 'I give 'im 'is ten bob note back so 'e made eight shillin's profit!'

[104]

Our concentration now broken, the cricket match lost its appeal. We made our tortuous way home, me walking on the front garden walls of the houses while Albie hopped, skipped and staggered along the pavement avoiding the land mines which were planted in the cracks between the paving stones and which would blow your feet off if you landed on one.

'What we gonna do now?' Albie enquired.

'Do! What d'you think we're gonna do? We're gonna take this money to your Mam before you starts feelin' like an ice-cream again!'

We approached Albie's back door with some trepidation. Before we got a foot over the doorstep his Mam came flying out with an armful of washing and a mouthful of clothes pegs.

Without stopping to draw breath and without dropping a single peg she abused Albie between her clenched teeth. 'What time d'you reckon this is to come 'ome for your tea? Where in the devil 'ave you bin? I've told you to keep away from 'im! Jus' look at the colour o' your jersey, clean on this mornin'! You look as if you'd been dragged through an 'edge backwards! Don't stand there gawpin', jus' let that washin' line down for me!'

''Scuse, me – er – Mrs – er –,' I began.

'Gerrout of 'ere an' gerroff 'ome,' she snapped.

'We got somethin' for you,' I persisted.

'Well, I ain't got nothin' for you, so 'op off before I puts my foot be'ind you,' she answered, most ungratefully.

'It's only two an' tuppence ha'penny, but it's nearly 'alf what you gotta get to pay the 'lectric.'

'What've you bin tellin' ev'rybody?' she screamed at Albie, cuffing his ear with a hand as hard as a rock. 'We don't want our business gabbled up an' down the street.'

'I ain't the street,' I protested. 'I'm jus' me!'

She ignored me and knocked Albie's head back up straight with a back hander to his other ear. 'Goin' an' tellin' 'im, of all people! It'll be all over the town in no time, once 'is mother knows. She've got a trap on 'er like Cheddar Gorge!'

I was about to plunge to the defence of my mother's mouth when I became aware of sounds emanating from Albie's house which by rights should not have been possible.

'What's that?'

'What's what?'

'That noise.'

'That noise, I'll 'ave you know, is "In Town Tonight".'

'On the wireless?'

'Well it don't come out o' the sewin' machine!'

'Don't your wireless run off the 'lectric?'

'No, it uses 'ot air! Course it runs off the 'lectric.'

'But – I thought – Albie said –'

'It must've bin switched on again,' suggested Albie from his hiding-place behind the shed.

'Course it's bin switched on again! Di'n't think I was goin' to miss me Sat'day night Music 'all, did you?'

'But 'ow d'you do it?'

'Well, there was this 'orse in the two o'clock at Newmarket – Just Our Luck it was called – an' your Dad says it'd be just our luck if it went an' won an' we di'n't 'ave nothin' on it, so 'e borrows a tanner out o' the rent money an' goes an' puts it on an' up it comes at fourteen to one so off 'e goes down the 'lectric board an' pays the bill an' gives this feller 'e knows a tanner to come round right away an' we was all turned on again by four o'clock. I thought I asked you to give me an 'and with this washing. Where've you got to now?'

By the time she paused to look round Albie and me were well on our way towards the corner shop.

'Two an' tuppence ha'penny,' breathed Albie rapturously. 'We c'n 'ave ice-cream an' aniseed balls an' fruity chews an' extra strong mints an' a choc'late cream mouse an' –'

'An' still enough for some chips later on an' a bottle o' Tizer,' I added.

'We ain't never 'ad quite so much money to spend all at one go, 'ave we?'

'I don't reckon so,' I said seriously.

'An' all of it earned by our own 'ard work.'

Albie looked at me out of the corner of his eye.

'Well,' I said thoughtfully, 'there's all kinds of work, ain't there? You can 'ump bricks for a penny an hour an' you can shovel coal for a penny an hour. Or you can use your brains an' get two shillin's in less than two minutes. I don't think I fancy workin' down the shuntin' yard any more. I'm gonna concentrate on buildin' up me brains a bit more an' get a job where you earns thousands of pounds without workin'. I mean to say, I wouldn't *mind* workin', but you can't afford to reely, can you?'

I waited for his reply but none was forthcoming. 'You listenin' to me?' I demanded.

'I was jus' thinkin',' muttered Albie.

'Thinkin' what?'

'I was thinkin' – well, our Mam ain't 'alf gonna be mad when I gets 'ome again. D'you think we'll 'ave enough to buy 'er a quarter o' fruit drops for a sort of peace offerin'?'

What Are Little Girls Made of?

'We def'nitely ain't 'avin' no girls in our gang!' Albie announced. I had never heard him so angry. His cheeks burned red and he was quivering with temper. 'We kept 'em out till now so I don't see why she should be any diff'rent jus' 'cos she've moved in nex' door to you.'

But I felt different about Audrey. She *was* different. She was the first girl I ever met that saved fag cards, played marbles, knew about Arsenal and preferred Beechnut chewing gum to dolly mixtures.

'But she ain't like other girls,' I protested. 'I mean – she ain't an ordin'ry, dopey girl like all the others up our street, is she?'

'She's a girl,' said Albie, closing the subject.

We were sitting on the old canal bridge in our best Sunday togs, while Bonzo, my Auntie Hilda's dog, scrabbled around below us on the tow-path, diving in and out of the reeds and retrieving old bits of wood and broken bedsteads and bicycle wheels and other junk which people had been depositing in the canal for the last fifty years or more. Ever since the railways had taken over from the barges, the old canal had become a dumping ground, a filthy mess of stagnant water, a disgusting place to grown-ups and absolute heaven to small boys and mongrel dogs.

Bonzo was a super mongrel. He must have comprised a bit of just about every breed of dog that ever existed. He was as black as night (come to think of it, he was probably put together in the dark, he was such an odd mixture). He looked like a sort of black red setter with wiry hair, terrier-type ears, a scrubbing-brush tail and enormous plates of meat big enough to muck up a carpet or a kitchen floor in next to no time. He was a rare beauty.

We sat and watched him slurping through the mud, making all kinds of exciting discoveries – a wheel-less pram, a rusty mangle, a tin chest, a front door (how did that get there?).

'What time's yer tea?' Albie asked.

'Usual. Five o'clock Sundays,' I replied, chipping bits of cement out of the bridge with the metal protector my Dad always nailed into the heel of my shoe.

'Ours is early today,' said Albie. 'Me Gramp's comin' fer tea.'

'Ain't you lucky,' I said. I knew what Albie's Gramp coming to tea meant. Afterwards he and Albie's Dad would take Albie and his two younger brothers round to the British Legion club and sit them in the passage while the men played dominoes, sending them out bottles of ginger beer and fizzy lemonade at regular intervals till chucking-out time. I loved fizzy lemonade. I would have sat in any passage, anywhere, all night if necessary, for a bottle of fizzy lemonade. 'I better be off.' Albie drew his legs up on to the parapet and eased himself down on to the hump-backed bridge. 'See you tomorrow, eh?'

'Yeah!' I nodded. 'See you tomorrow, Albie.'

Tomorrow. Monday. School. The week-ends seemed to last hardly any time at all. It wasn't fair really, five days work and only two days off. The other way round would be a much fairer way of organising life.

Bonzo was nowhere to be seen. But someone else was. Coming along the tow-path was a small figure. As it got nearer, hopping, skipping and throwing stones into the water, it was clearly a girl. Immediately disinterested, I turned away.

'Bet you wouldn't jump off the bridge into the water,' challenged the girl.

I looked round. It was Audrey. She looked smashing with her coal-black, tousled hair framing her grubby round face, her tatty dress with torn pockets and fraying hem reaching unevenly to the scarred and bruised knees which protruded from her filthy wellies.

'What you all dressed up like a dog's dinner for, then?' she enquired, hoisting herself up on the parapet.

'It's Sunday, ennit,' I replied. Sunday seemed to be the cause of a great many of my problems.

'What about Sunday?' Audrey tucked her wellies up under her so they wouldn't fall in the canal, which they might well have done if she had dangled her legs, seeing they were about three sizes too big for her. 'What's the difference 'tween bein' up the cut on a Sunday an' a Sat'day? You don' 'ave to wear your best clothes to sit 'ere jus' 'cos it's Sunday, do you?'

'Our Mam don't know I'm up the cut, do she?' I answered her with a scathing glance.

'Where you s'posed to be, then, all dolled up in them posh clothes?' she persisted.

I didn't really want to tell her, but you know how it is with some people, you just seem to have to spill it all out. 'Up the cemet'ry,' I muttered.

'Eh?' Audrey thrust her face close to mine. 'Can't you speak no louder 'n that? You got summat up with you?'

'Cemet'ry,' I yelled in her earhole. She drew back, a

little hurt. I stared furiously down into the murky water below.

Audrey, like I said to Albie, was not to be numbered among ordinary girls, She didn't give up easily. She returned to the attack with a flourish.

''Oo d'you know up the cemet'ry?'

'Well, you don't ackchully *know* people up the cemet'ry, do you? I mean – well – you can't say you knows 'em if they're up there. I mean to say.' Audrey started to giggle.

'Well, if you mus' know,' I concluded with some dignity. 'It's my Great Uncle Alf.'

Audrey pondered while I awaited the obvious retort.

'What's the diff'rence 'tween an ordin'ry uncle an' a great one?'

'If 'e's great,' I informed her in the tone of voice Mr Clements used if I asked him a daft question at school. 'If 'e's great, then it means 'e's better'n jus' an ordinary uncle, dunnit? 'S obvious, ennit?'

''Oo said 'e was great?'

'Our Gran. 'E was summat to do with 'er. But 'e died 'fore I was born so I never seen 'im. I takes flowers up 'is grave ev'ry Christmas an' on 'is birthday. A present from Gran, like.'

'Where are they then?' She certainly asked a lot of questions. A bit like old Fanny Flopdrawers that kept the post office. Perhaps Audrey was more of a girl than I had suspected, in spite of her scruffy, tom-boy appearance.

'Where's what?' I asked wearily.

'The flowers for your Great Uncle Thingummy.'

'I already took 'em. I took 'em first so as I could c'lect Bonzo on the way back an' take 'im for a walk.'

''Oo's Bonzo?'

I gestured vaguely in the direction of the tow-path.

[111]

'I can't see nothin',' said Audrey.

And when I got round to looking – I couldn't see anything either.

'Well, 'e was there. A minute ago. We was watchin' 'im, me an' Albie. 'E was down there, discov'rin' things.'

''E ain't there now, is 'e? Whatever 'e is!'

''E's a dog. The greates' dog what ever lived.' I began making dog-attracting noises. 'C'mon, Bonzo! C'm'ere, boy! Bonzy, bonzy!'

'I s'pose ev'rybody you knows is great,' Audrey said quietly. 'Great Uncle Thingummy and now Great Dog Bonzo.'

''E is great,' I hissed, but there was as much fear as anger in my voice. 'Bonzo! Where are you, Bonzo?' If only he would stick his black tail up out of the reeds like a periscope – or start making wuffling noises like he did when he discovered something exciting. 'Bonzo! C'mon, boy! Tea-time!' He couldn't have – oh, please God, no! Not that! Surely, he'd have made a noise of some sort. 'Bonzy! Bonzy, Bonzy, Bonzy!'

I stood on the parapet, shading my eyes against the late afternoon sun. Please, please, show me a sign, I prayed. I'll dive in if it will do any good, even with my best jersey on. Anything. Only please let him be all right. Because if he isn't it's sure to be my fault because everything that ever happens is always my fault, and our Auntie Hilda will never forgive me because he means so much to her since Uncle Will went off and left her. And I don't want Bonzo to die, either. Not to drown in that rotten old canal with me sitting here not even noticing what was happening. All because of that stupid girl.

''Ave 'e got a black 'ead,' the stupid girl cried out. 'Like a sort of woolly sea-lion with ears? 'Cos if 'e 'as – there 'e 'is!'

[112]

She pointed to a clump of reeds about a hundred yards off towards the blood and bone yard. At first I couldn't see anything, but when Audrey caught my arm and dragged me across to where she stood, balanced precariously on the narrow parapet, the wider angle enabled me to see Bonzo's head sticking unmistakably out of the water, behind the reeds and several feet out from the bank.

I closed my eyes in another rare burst of silent prayer. I could almost – well, not quite, but if she had been a boy I would certainly – have patted Audrey's shoulder.

As I scrambled down the loose earth steps to the tow-path I was suddenly beset with fresh fears. Why hadn't I heard Bonzo barking? There was no wind to carry the sound away. And Bonzo's bark would have carried a great deal more than a hundred yards if he really let rip.

I ran full pelt along the hard, narrow path, the long grass whipping my bare knees on either side. And Audrey, despite her size six wellies, was not far behind.

'Bonzo!' I cried as I ran. 'Comin', boy. I'm comin', Bonzo dog.'

'An' me,' I heard Audrey call breathlessly, either to comfort me or Bonzo – or both of us.

When I was still twenty paces short of him I could hear Bonzo whining, a kind of high-pitched whimper unlike any noise I'd ever heard him make before. He was a couple of yards or so out from the bank, only his head above water, although occasionally his tail would break the surface with a pathetic flick.

'Bonzo, it's me,' I called to him, quite uselessly. He began to thrash about below the water. His whining grew more shrill, more urgent.

''E's gonna drown,' I sobbed.

''E ain't,' pronounced Audrey. ''E's gonna strangle. If we don't get to 'im quick.'

[113]

And without further thought – either for her life, her clothes, her parents – all the things I usually considered before taking desperate remedies – she jumped off the tow-path into the reeds and the slime and began to wade out to the dog.

Bonzo turned his big, frightened eyes towards her. 'It's all right,' she soothed. 'It's only me, Audrey.' And while I dithered on the brink, she turned, as if reading my mind, and said: 'Don't you go muckin' up them fancy clothes o' yourn. Wait there an' see if I can manage meself.'

It was deeper than I thought. She was up over her wellingtons in no time. When she reached out to touch Bonzo's head the water was lapping at the hem of her dress.

Bonzo's natural reaction to strangers was to bite them. Not hard – but enough to show that he was not a dog to be messed about with. And so, notwithstanding the fact that Audrey went out to rescue him, Bonzo snapped.

'Don't be daft,' Audrey scolded him. 'I'm tryin' to 'elp.'

'E's goin' under,' I screeched as Bonzo's nose dipped below the surface.

''E's all caught up in this wire,' Audrey shouted, bending to get her arms under Bonzo's body to support him. 'It's all round 'is neck an' legs. I c'n feel it round my legs, as well. There mus' be miles of it.'

Oh, crikey, I thought – very near panic – if she goes and gets herself all tangled up and there's the *two* of them, both drowning! It was time for action. I plunged into the slimey, oozey, squelchy, black mud.

''Old me 'and!'

Audrey thrust out a grubby paw, and after only a split second's hesitation, I took hold of it. Well, I mean

[114]

to say, it *was* a matter of life and death and there was nobody looking. I shuddered to think what Albie would have said. Or any of the rest of the gang. Actually holding a girl's hand in my own. And holding it very firmly, too, as Audrey put most of her weight on to me as she thrust her other hand under the water and began to free her legs of the entangling wire.

'You get an 'old on Bonzo,' she ordered, letting go my hand and straightening up. There was no doubt who was in charge of operations. Proper little foreman she'd make. I sloshed forward into deeper water – up over the hem of my short trousers – and grabbed Bonzo by his collar.

'You don't 'ave to strangle 'im any more than what the wire's doin',' Audrey remonstrated. 'I only said for you to 'old 'im 'cos 'e knows you better 'n me an' you can calm 'im down while I tries to undo 'im from all this wire.'

She had both her arms under the murky water now, right up to her armpits, tugging and bending and twisting, while I tried to free the dog's head of the rusty loops of wire which were buried deep in his coat and already cutting into his flesh. And all the while I was calming the dog: 'Good boy! Still, now. That's it. Lovely lad!' and Audrey was calming me! 'Keep a good 'old on 'im. Talk to 'im, then! That's better. It's comin'.'

Goodness knows what idiot had dumped this lot in the cut. As Audrey said, there seemed to be miles of it. Enough to replace all the telephone lines from here to kingdom come, as my mother would have said.

I got my first two fingers under the loop which was threatening to choke poor old Bonzo. I got the dog's chest wedged between my knees to support him so that I could bring both hands to bear on the task of easing the noose over his head.

[115]

'Careful, dopey!' Audrey warned me. 'Don't pull too 'ard. That bit's joined on to the bit I got 'old of an' it goes all round 'is back legs.'

'But I've nearly got 'is 'ead free,' I protested, bending Bonzo's floppy ears tight against his skull. 'Once 'e've got 'is 'ead free 'e'll feel a lot better.'

Audrey appeared to see the point of this and we soon had four hands dealing with the front end of the dog. Bonzo, at last sensing that we were trying to save him and not finish him off, leaned his weight against my legs, quietly treading water and gazing into my face with that strangely innocent, wide-eyed, trusting look that only a dog can achieve.

'Got it!' I yelled triumphantly – and promptly sat back in two feet of mud and water.

'Crikey!' said Audrey. 'You ain't 'alf in a muck!'

'I c'n see that, can't I,' I bawled. 'I don't need you to tell me I've gone an' mucked up me best Sunday trousers. I dunno what's gonna 'appen when I gets 'ome.'

I had a pretty good idea what would happen and the thought of it brought tears to my eyes!

'Never mind about it now,' Audrey said soothingly. 'We ain't finished rescuin' 'im yet.'

Bonzo was still trapped by his back legs and his rear end was thrashing furiously around spraying muck far and wide. 'Stop messin' about,' Audrey ordered, thumping Bonzo on his great, black dome with her little fist. 'We're doin' our best. Now stand still a mo.'

The dog, recognising the tone of authority in the voice, meekly obeyed. Audrey dipped her arms once more into the murky depths and recommenced rescue operations. As I was now nearly obliterated by mud – I looked like I was wearing more mud than clothes – I decided I might as well forget the troubles that lay ahead and help Audrey finish the job. I put my arms under Bonzo's body and lifted him off the canal bed.

'That's it!' panted Audrey, her arms flailing away below water-level like Tarzan's mate wrestling with an alligator.

Only I didn't feel too much like Tarzan.

''Old 'im there,' she demanded. 'Keep 'im steady. Good boy!'

I wasn't sure whether the last two words were for me or the dog, but I decided that they must have been meant for me and I cheered up quite perceptibly and felt just a shade more like the Tarzan of the Saturday flicks!

'Got it!'

''Ave you?'

'Jus' one more loop an' 'e's free.'

'Good dog. 'Old on a tick. Good boy.'

''Ere it comes!'

With a final grunt and a heave, Audrey came up with her arms entangled in endless loops of rusty wire. Bonzo, in gratitude, lashed her with his soggy tail, then kicked out for the bank giving us a final spraying of top quality canal water.

''Elp me out,' Audrey demanded, offering me her hand once again. I hesitated. But it was such a filthy, normal, boyish sort of hand that there didn't seem to be any harm in taking hold of it. I had a quick peek up and down the bank to make sure nobody could see my second contact with a female hand, then grabbed it fiercely and pulled her after me into the weed and sludge and thence on to the tow-path.

'Crikey!' I groaned. 'You ain't 'alf in a mess.'

'Pot callin' kettle black.' She pointed at me. 'Looks like we both been rollin' on the beach at Weston when the tide's out!'

'What we gonna do?' I asked weakly.

I had a feeling she would know. Being a woman. Maybe only a girl-woman but I felt instinctively that she would be able to think like my Mum. She'd know what we ought to do. Or say. Or something.

After a few moments' deliberation, she said, 'We better go over the rec. 'fore we goes 'ome.'

'The rec!' I replied, incredulous, flicking globs of mud off my socks and shoes. 'That's the daftest idea I ever 'eard. What do we wanna go to the recreation ground for in this state?'

My confidence in her was fast ebbing away.

''Cos, dopey,' she said gently, like a mother hen scolding a wayward chick, 'they got a public lavvy over there, ain't they? An' there's a sink what you can 'ave a wash in. Leastways – there is in the Ladies' 'alf. I 'spect there is in the Gents', ain't there?'

I can't say I'd ever noticed. But I could always go in the Ladies' end when there was nobody about while Audrey kept watch.

'That's a good idea,' I said admiringly.

Audrey beamed. Her face lit up. She looked like a scruffier edition of the girl in the Bisto Kids adverts.

'We won't be able to get you as clean as what you was when you started out 's afternoon but we'll be able to wash off some o' the worst.'

'Let's take Bonzo 'ome first,' I suggested. 'Then we can see to me.'

Audrey looked a little hurt.

'An' me,' she remonstrated, 'I got a bit mucked up as well.'

She scooped a fistful of mud off her dress, rolled it into a ball and hurled it across the width of the canal.

We set off along the path back towards town. Bonzo, his recent frightening dabble with death already forgotten, dashed happily in and out of the reeds, occasionally nuzzling Audrey's wellies to prove that she had been accepted as one of us.

''E ain't 'alf in a state,' said my Auntie Hilda when we eventually arrived at her house. 'You ain't been up that filthy old canal with 'im, 'ave you?'

'No!' we lied together.

'You look a bit of a muck yourself,' Auntie Hilda did one of her disgusted sniffs. Haven't you got no decent clothes to wear on a Sunday?'

How could I tell her that these were my best clothes? Leastways, they were an hour or so ago!

'And who's that you got with you?' She peered at Audrey who was standing by the front gate picking bits off the privet hedge and flicking them at Bonzo. 'You certainly has some odd friends.'

Auntie Hilda gave an even more disapproving sniff, patted the two great buns of grey hair that were skewered over her earholes and turned to go inside.

'I was going to give you one o' me cherry cakes but I don't reckon you deserve it,' she called over her shoulder. 'And I don't think you need bother to call next Sunday. C'mon, Bonzo. Looks like another bath day for you!'

'What's up with ol' Missus Misery-guts?' Audrey asked as we trudged across the deserted recreation ground. 'I wouldn't take 'er bloomin' dog out for 'er if that's 'ow she carries on when 'e gets a bit wet.'

'Well, 'e was more 'n a bit wet, really, I s'pose,' I said. 'Auntie 'ilda's all right, usually. An' 'er cherry cakes is great. When you gets one, that is!'

I quickly established that the reason I had never noticed a wash basin in the Gents' was because it had obviously been wrenched off the wall and either pinched or smashed up years ago. So we decided on a plan of action.

[119]

'I'll go an' get meself a bit spruced,' said Audrey, who wasn't as bothered as I was because she wasn't wearing her best clobber anyway and she hadn't been all that clean to start with. 'An' then I'll keep guard while you 'as a bit of a wash.'

She reappeared after about two minutes looking exactly the same, except that where she had been plastered with dried mud it was now all freshened up again into wet mud.

'Ain't no towel there no more,' she explained. 'Somebody bin an' broke the roller bit off. An' the mirror's all smashed. But the water's all right. Only a little trickle, but it's all right. 'Cept you can't fill the sink 'cos the plug's gone!'

From long and very painful experience I had learned that dried mud is best left alone and then brushed off when you get home (if you can creep in and get hold of the clothes brush off the hook in the passage without beeing seen, that is). So I just tried to wash off my shoes and my knees and hands. Three times I had to rush out when Audrey's piercing whistle warned of approaching females who might be heading for the lavatory. The third time I gave up.

'You don't look any diff'rent,' said Audrey inspecting me up and down. 'Them shoes is so wet I shouldn't think they'll never get dry again. An' the lace 'oles is bunged up wi' mud. An' you can't really tell where your shoes ends an' your socks starts. An' your face is all streaky –'

'Shurrup!' was all I could say, and I set off home – cold, wet and fed up – with Audrey trailing ten yards behind.

'Lot o' thanks I gets,' I could hear her nattering to herself as she mooched along, clacking a stick against the park railings. 'Anybody 'd think it was all my fault.

[120]

'E wasn't my dog, was 'e? Don't matter what you does for some people . . .'

Sounded exactly like my Mum, my Gran, my Auntie Doll, Mrs Next-door Barratt and all the other women I'd had on my back for the last goodness knows how long.

She caught me up on the corner of our street. 'What you gonna do?' she asked quietly.

'Do?' I howled, the tears welling up in my eyes in anticipation of my Dad's hand in about two minutes from now. 'I'm goin' 'ome, that's what. I'm already hours late fer me tea an' what with all this mud an' everythin' . . .'

I turned away from her before I let myself down completely by snivelling in front of a girl. I could hear her squelching along behind me in her huge wellies as I kicked open the back gate and crossed the yard.

'Oh my God!' my Mother said when I walked in the scullery. I could have bet what she would say next. 'Dad! Come 'ere this instant an' look at this son o' yourn!'

My Dad came. He looked. He said nothing. I hoped he had been struck speechless. But no such luck. He recovered himself. He spoke so soft it was more like thinking than speaking. And the more quiet he spoke the worse it was going to be for me. I had good reason to know!

'Is that what I goes to work for? To keep you in clothes so as you can go up that bloomin' canal an' plaster yourself with muck. On a Sunday, an' all!'

He took a couple of paces forward, down the step from the sitting-room into the scullery. Now for it. There was no escape. The sooner he started clouting me ear the sooner it would be over. I shut my eyes.

''E ain't 'alf brave, mister,' said a small voice behind me.

My Dad held his ground. He used the hand that was upraised to belt me to take the cigarette out of his mouth.

[121]

'Oh! An' who might you be?' he asked.

'She's Audrey,' my Mother said, recognising her even under the layers of canal mud. 'She's the new people's girl from next door.'

'Is she indeed! Well, she've come to the wrong 'ouse, then, ain't she?'

'I bin with 'im.' Audrey pointed at me. 'An' I seen ev'rythin'. 'E's the bravest rescuer I ever seen. 'E jumped in the cut with all 'is clothes on to save this dog what was drownin'. Never stopped to think about 'isself, 'e di'n't. Jus' jumped in an' swum right out to this dog . . .'

'Swam? 'E swam?' my Dad interrupted.

Audrey backed down cleverly. I couldn't have done better myself.

'Well, 'e *looked* as if 'e was swimmin'. If 'e wasn't, it makes it braver, don't it? Jumpin' in like that an' not knowin' 'ow deep it was an' not bein' able to swim! Well, 'e looked as if 'e was swimmin'. 'E must 'ave been walkin' on the bottom with the water right up to 'is chin!'

My mother suddenly threw her arms around me and clutched me to her Sunday pinny. 'Oh Dad!' she sobbed. 'We nearly lost 'im in the canal!'

My Dad didn't look too impressed. He knew me better than my mother. He'd never rated me as much of a hero.

'The dog's all right, too,' Audrey said to cover the silence.

'I'm glad about that,' my Dad replied, sarcastic like. 'Must 'ave been a bit of a job knowin' which was the dog an' which was 'im when they come out the water!'

My Mum gave me another paralysing hug. Audrey reached out and squeezed my arm. My Dad – up against two females – gave up the unequal contest and returned to his armchair and Radio Luxembourg.

I could hardly wait to get round Albie's house on the Monday morning.

'Don't alter the fact she's a girl, do it?' he said after I had told him about Audrey's courageous performance with Bonzo.

'But I keep tellin' you, nobody could've done it better,' I persisted. And then – the final accolade – 'I tell you what, Albie, she was the one what went in first.'

He looked at me with a mixture of disbelief and contempt. 'You let 'er go in first? You mean she went in to rescue 'im 'fore you did?'

'Yeah!' I said defiantly. 'I'm glad it was 'er there with me an' not you!'

Albie thought that over for a minute and before he could come back with an answer, I went on: 'An' she went 'ome with me an' told our Dad 'ow I saved Bonzo, an' it wasn't my fault I was all covered in mud an' spoilt me Sunday shoes an' me best socks. An' 'e never touched me!'

'You mean you went wadin' down the cut an' your ol' man never clouted you one?'

''S true. She told 'im what I'd done an' 'e just sort o' went quiet an' sat in 'is chair an' never spoke again all night.'

'Crikey!' said Albie, choked with admiration. 'She mus' be good if she can do that! Rescuin' dogs in the canal is pretty good but if she can keep your Dad's 'air on when you gets 'ome in that state . . . at that time . . . on a Sunday . . .'

Albie's admiration left him without adequate words to express himself. He was silent all the way down Corporation Street till we got to the school gate. Then he turned to me and said, 'Nex' Sunday we'll take Bonzo up Ladder Lane an' see if there's any blackberries out yet. Shall we? We'll go straight away after dinner, eh? You an' me an' Bonzo' – he looked me squarely in the eye – 'An' Audrey, if you like.'

[123]

The Autograph

'Can I 'ave yer pass-out, mister?'

The man drew his overcoat collar higher round his ears and hurried away into the late November afternoon mist, ignoring me and my question. The heavy timber gate slammed shut. I huddled against it, my numb fingers clenched inside my trouser pockets. The roar of the crowd swelled up again from the other side of the fence. I pressed my face against the cold, damp wood. Was it a goal? For us? Or a near miss? Or a penalty?

The last time the score had filtered through, Town were winning two-one. And we badly needed a win. Many more defeats and we'd be back on the bottom of the Third Division (South) and having to apply for re-election to the league like we did in '32-'33. And one of these years we'd be voted out and that would be the end of football at the County Ground and I wouldn't be able to spend Saturday afternoons begging for a pass-out to get in and see the second half. And if that happened I would die.

The crowd started baying and howling again. Was somebody getting sent off? And me missing it! Sendings off nearly always happened in the second half. I loved them. It made my stomach turn over – a rare mixture of cold dread and high excitement – when the referee pointed his finger and a lonely criminal trudged off down the tunnel to the dressing-room. I wanted to get my marching orders when I grew up and became a pro – to take that long walk, alone, and get suspended and have my photo on the back page of the *Daily Herald*.

I heard the first squeak of the thick, greasy bolt being drawn back again. Another muffled-up figure slipped through the gate and rushed off to catch an early bus or eat an early tea. Fancy paying to see a football match and not stopping to the full-time whistle!

'Please, mister, can I 'ave yer pass-out?'

'Sorry, son. Di'n't know they 'ad pass-outs.'

I settled back to my vigil.

All the other lads were inside now, except me. All clustered against the boards behind the goal at the town end. Wondering where I'd got to, probably. I didn't want to deprive them of anything, but I hoped there wouldn't be any more goals until I got there.

There were about ten of us. And we had a system. A strict rota. This week I was last. Next week I'd be first in the queue again. The first pass-outs were issued at half-time. Some people took them because they intended coming back. (But where did they go?) Others refused them and raced off to wherever they had to go. But there were a few, mostly bus drivers and engine crew on shift work, who knew we'd be waiting outside and they took their pass-outs and slipped them to us as they came by. And we would solemnly kick the gate and present our little pink tickets to Lanky Charlie, the gateman, who would equally solemnly tear them in half and usher us into the Holy Land.

Years later I got to wondering why on earth Charlie couldn't just have opened the gate at half-time and let us all in at one go. Anybody would have thought the chairman of the board of directors was going round counting the number of extra small boys who weren't there before half-time!

The big double gates were suddenly swung wide open.

'C'mon, then, tiddler,' said Lanky Charlie, fixing the gates back with heavy iron bars. 'Ten minutes to go an' it's two each.'

The gates were always opened ten minutes from the end ready for the rush when the whistle blew, and any of us who had not managed to nab a pass-out could go in then.

'Where you bin?' asked Albie as I shoved my way towards them.

'We're drawin' two-two,' Vic said sadly. 'You missed a goal.'

''Ow long is there left?'

'It's the last ten minutes,' I said. 'Lanky Charlie's opened the gates.'

'We'll never win now,' moaned Spud. 'We ain't won at 'ome since September an' we ain't goin' to win agen!'

Through the gloom and mist (my Dad would have said football under floodlights was story-book stuff in those days), I could dimly make out the action at the far end of the field. Around our goal. As usual.

'Please, God, don't let their lot score again,' muttered Albie, hands together, eyes closed.

An *aagh* from the scattering of supporters on the ash bank behind the distant goal signalled a near miss. The resultant goal-kick set the Town on the attack. Tommy Walters, Town's outside right, bore down on us with the ball at his feet.

'Come on, Tommy,' we yelled. 'Shoot, Tommy!'

In answer to our advice, Tommy drew back his right

foot, but before he could complete the movement, his leg was hooked away and he crashed spectacularly in the mud.

'Penalty!' I screeched. 'Penalty, ref!'

There was a heart-stopping moment of indecision and then – oh joy – the shrill blast, the pointing finger, the relieved cries from the spectators, the rapture and the agony of the players.

The visiting team went bonkers. They argued with the referee – they rushed over to plead with the lines-man – they spat in the mud. Tommy Walters placed the ball carefully on the twelve yard spot. Their centre-half – a hulking, hairy-legged brute with a parting like a tram-line down the centre of his smooth, short-cropped, black hair – strode up and moved the ball back six inches.

'Take 'is name,' we yelled. 'Take 'is name!'

The ref, taking our advice to heart, brought his notebook out of his blazer pocket with a flourish.

''E's bookin' 'im!' I was delirious with the ecstasy and the drama.

The big footballer towered over the official, still arguing, gesticulating and – my heart turned over in my chest like a small football!

''E've sent 'im off!'

'Gerroff, yer big stiff.'

Baring his teeth, swearing and spitting, the offender began his lonely trudge towards the tunnel. I was with him every plodding step of the way, trying to capture his feelings. How long did the anger last? Was he sorry now? What would his manager say? What would it be like back there in the dressing-room, alone in the steaming, communal bath?

'To 'is left, Tommy,' Spud shouted. 'Put it to 'is left!'

I dragged my thoughts back from the lonely

dressing-room as Tommy Walters began his swerving run. He feinted to do as Spud suggested and put the ball to the left of the crouching goalie, then thumped it hard and true into the opposite corner. I ducked instinctively as the huge, muddy ball thunked into the net directly in front of my face.

'Three-two,' screamed Vic. 'We've won.'

''Old yer 'orses,' said the lugubrious policeman who always stood near the goal to see none of us sat on the boards with our legs dangling over the other side. 'There's another five minutes to go, yet.'

But we held out for the five minutes, with Albie and Vic and Spud and me and the rest of our gang and the other five thousand all sweating as much as the players on the field.

'Got yer book?' asked Albie, as soon as the last red jersey had disappeared down the tunnel and left us stamping our frozen feet on the fast-emptying terrace.

'Yeah. You got yours?'

Albie nodded.

We were the only two in the gang who were auto-graph addicts. After every game we would make our way round the back of the big stand to the red-painted door with its neat little message, 'Players and Officials only.' There would be perhaps twenty or thirty kids there, half of whom would disappear long before the statutory thirty minutes which it took the visiting players to bathe, dress, drink whatever it was football-ers drank after matches, and make their appearance in twos and threes and stroll down the main street to the railway station which was fifteen minutes' walk away. If they'd taken two hours Albie and I would have still been there!

We joined in the game of 'three and in' with a couple of lads we'd seen there before, one of whom owned the best tennis ball I'd ever played football with. It was so new it still had hair on it!

''Ere they come,' the cry went up. We watched our beloved idols as they came out on to the stage we created for them.

'Good ol' Tommy,' said Albie, who wasn't a bit shy. 'That was a clinkin' penalty!'

Tommy Walters, Sid Armstrong, Wally Davidson, Sandy Gilliver – we touched their sleeves as they hurried past as a mark of respect. We'd got all their autographs long since. It was the visitors we were after.

There was always an interval between the departure of the home side and the emergence of the visitors – I used to think it was a clever plan by the management to keep the players from carrying on their personal battles in the street.

When the other lot eventually appeared, we rushed them with our books open at a fresh, pink page and our newly-sharpened school pencils at the ready.

'Can I 'ave yer autograph, please, mister?'

We knew which ones to ask – the young ones, freshly-bathed with slicked down hair and long belted overcoats, carrying brown leather bags. The old men in black coats and trilby hats were directors and hangers-on.

'Are you the goalie? I thought you played great! Will you sign me book – please?'

They weren't happy, this lot. Still fretting over that penalty and the lost bonus. They pushed past us and strode off towards the station. But we were persistent little beggars. We ran ahead of them, got under their feet and badgered them until they mostly signed in self-defence. By the time we had pestered them to the station approach, I had all of them in my little, green, suede-covered book except one. The big bloke who had been sent off wouldn't sign for any of us. He mooched along, head down, apart from the rest of his mates, ignoring all our approaches.

'We'll never get 'im. I'm goin' 'ome,' sighed Albie. 'You comin'?'

'Don't chicken out, Albie,' I coaxed him. 'We gotta get all eleven of 'em.'

'I got twelve already,' said Albie.

'You must've got the trainer an' the manager. They don't count.'

'I'm goin'.' Albie turned away. 'We got beans on toast today.'

I was starving, too – but my stubborn streak won out over the hunger pangs. I stalked my quarry right into the station booking hall.

I shoved my book into his chest once more. 'Please, mister. I'm sorry you got sent off. I seen plenty o' players do worse 'n what you done an' get away with it.'

He noticed me for the first time.

'I got all the others 'cept you. An' it won't count if I don't get the full team!'

There was a long moment of indecision. The other players brushed past us and surged away up the steps to number one platform.

Then he handed me his bag and took my little book in his huge fist. I still have the invisible imprint of the warm, smooth, leather handle across my palm; can still feel the surprising weight of it (there must have been a hundredweight of mud clinging to the boots, jersey, knicks and socks which were hidden in its depths). He held the book against the platform ticket machine and wrote laboriously. I didn't mind if it took him an hour – I was actually holding a real, professional footballer's bag in my bloodless, tingling fingers.

[130]

We exchanged bag for book.

'Thank you, mister,' I breathed.

He never spoke. I watched him bound up the steps three at a time and melt into the mist and smoke.

'Yer tea's in the dustbin,' my mother greeted me when I arrived home, breathless. She always said it if anyone came in late for a meal. But I knew it would be in the oven keeping warm. Bubble and squeak, probably, a bit dried up and burned round the edge from waiting too long for me.

'Bin playin' extra time or summat?' said my Dad from behind the racing results.

'I got 'em all,' I said proudly, shoving my book over the top of his paper. 'I was the only one as got 'em all.'

I went out in the scullery and took the red-hot plate out of the oven with my bare hands, my fingers so numb with cold I didn't feel the pain till half a minute later.

My Dad began to laugh. He didn't laugh too much in those days. It was a thin, dry crackle. 'What sort of game did Donald Duck 'ave?' he wheezed.

'Who?'

He held the open book out to me. At the bottom of the page, under the genuine scrawls and squiggles, was written DONALD DUCK in crude, printed capitals.

I fled upstairs. I lay on my bed and with my chunky, green rubber I erased the two words with such thoroughness that what with the pressure and the dampness from a couple of stray tears, I pretty nearly rubbed a hole in the paper.

'Did you get 'im?' asked Albie, first thing Monday morning in the playground.

'Who? Oh 'im!' I said nonchalantly. 'Naw, I never bothered. We 'ad bubble an' squeak for tea. Anyway, I looked in the Sunday paper an' 'e was only a reserve. Their first team centre-'alf was injured.'

'Honest?' Albie said brightly. 'We got all the ones that mattered, then. All the decent ones.'

'Yeah,' I said, 'we got all the decent ones.'

The Jommetry Lesson

Every Thursday, dead on twelve, just as the big school bell was about to ring and send us all scuttling home for our dinners, old Mr Sharpe would shove his mottled purple face round our classroom door.

Ignoring little Miss Armitage, our class teacher, who sat at her high desk with a perpetual worried frown furrowing her forehead, he would bark at us: 'What day is it?'

'Thursday, sir,' we answered with one voice.

'And what's Thursday mean?'

'Jommetry, two till three, sir.'

Jommetry was a branch of arithmetic you graduated to in Standard V. Those who managed to get into Standard VI before they were fourteen and compulsorily retired to work for a living, had to do aljibra. And there were rumours that the kids who passed the scholarship and went up the hill to the Grammar School had to study a fearful subject called triggernometry.

Jommetry was bad enough for me!

I hated Thursdays. I went to bed every Wednesday night hoping I'd wake up and find it was Friday. And I was scared stiff of Old Dickie Sharpe. More scared than of any teacher since I was at Queenstown Infants' and

Miss Baldrey used to wallop me with a slipper because I was hopeless at raffia.

I wasn't the only one who couldn't eat any dinner on a Thursday. Everybody, including Bert Fuller and Charlie Tuck, the two biggest bullies in our class, was petrified of Dickie Sharpe. I used to wonder how Big Ernie felt about Thursday afternoons. None of us knew how Ernie felt about anything. Or if he felt at all.

Ernie wasn't very bright. He wasn't bad enough to qualify for Standard Nought. Kids who couldn't read or write went into Lower Standard Nought when they came up from the infants' at seven. If they still couldn't read by the time they were ten, they moved into Upper Standard Nought and stayed there until they left school. Big Ernie must have been very close to Standard Nought. He was still reading books with more pictures than words when he got to Standard V, and the only writing he could do was copying off the blackboard. It wouldn't have been so bad if he'd been small and inconspicuous. But at thirteen years of age he was nearly six feet tall. Like a great bean-pole among a forest of pea-sticks.

Like a lot of big people, Ernie was very gentle. He was the victim of a terrible amount of scragging in the playground and he hardly ever got nasty. But worse than that was the way some of the teachers took it out on him in the classrom. Especially Dickie Sharpe.

Even Bert Fuller and Charlie Tuck, who used to make mincemeat of Ernie when they waylaid him along the cut on the way home from school, felt sorry for him when Dickie Sharpe started lashing him with his tongue like he did every Thursday afternoon.

'And what masterpiece have we concocted this afternoon?' he would say, smooth as velvet, bending low over Ernie's bent head and breathing beer fumes all over him. (We all reckoned he went boozing in the Jug and Bottle at the Locomotive Thursday dinner-times, specially to prepare for battle with our lot in the afternoon.)

'Triangle, sir,' said Ernie. He never used two words where one would do.

'Well, now. Fancy that!' The purple face would go even more purple as he whisked up Ernie's exercise book and held it aloft. 'Look at this, everybody. Behold a four-sided triangle!'

Ernie cringed in his desk. None of us looked at him. The back of my head began to ache because I knew what was coming to Ernie any moment.

'And did you draw this square triangle all by yourself?'

'Yes, sir.'

'Well, now, you can rub it out all by yourself!'

Then – thwack! Thwack! Dickie's massive hand, the thick, stumpy fingers hard and rigid, would clump the base of Ernie's skull. I knew the feeling. It had happened to me a few times. It was like being beheaded with a blunt chopper. Twice!

And afterwards it felt as if the Christ Church bell-ringers were practising a few changes inside your head.

On this particular Thursday, I remember we were doing Pythagoras. We often did him! I didn't know why then and I'm sure I don't know why now. You weren't supposed to know why – asking questions was strictly barred – you just did what you were told. Particularly if Dickie Sharpe was doing the telling.

Dickie was on his usual patrol up and down the gangways between the rows of desks, making cruel, sarcastic jibes about our various inabilities at drawing right-angled triangles. He padded up behind Ernie in his silent, rubber-soled, shiny, black boots.

How his eyes must have glinted when he saw Ernie's

pencil. Unsharpened pencils were bad enough – two clumps round the ear. Pencils with chewed ends were almost a capital offence – two clumps, a teeth-chattering shaking and stay in at playtime. But a stumpy pencil – a titchy dog-end of pencil – that was the absolute limit.

Ernie's stub of pencil was so short you could only just see the end of it between his thumb and first finger as he struggled to complete his drawing.

'Well, now, what have we here?'

Ernie looked up, his great cow's eyes uncomprehending.

We all trembled in our dual desks.

'The workman is only as good as his tool,' cooed Dickie as if he was the most cultured and kindliest of teachers. 'And when did you discover this mighty implement?'

He removed the offending stub from Ernie's grubby hand.

'It's me pencil, sir.'

'Really?' murmured Dickie, sarcastic but still silky. 'Well, fancy that. Look at this, everybody. Does any boy know what this is?'

Silence.

'I'm not surprised. Not a bit surprised. But –' his voice began to rise and he took Ernie's left ear in his right hand – 'we have a clever lad here who thinks he knows what it is.' He tweaked the ear. 'What is it again?'

'Me pencil, sir.'

Then Dickie blew up. We were relieved in a funny sort of way. It was almost better to see his violence than to suffer his sarcasm.

'You dare to come to my jommetry lesson with a – with a – coalman's pencil!' He couldn't have been more venomous if it had been a time bomb.

We were all of us near fainting in fearful anticipation of what was to happen to the unfortunate Ernie for having dared to come to jommetry with a coalman's pencil. One of the reasons for Dickie's visit to our classroom at twelve o'clock on Thursdays was to remind us that a full-length, unchewed, needle-sharp pencil was the number one requirement for a trouble-free Thursday afternoon.

'Come here!' growled Dickie. Which was a bit unnecessary seeing that he had a firm grip on Ernie's ear and consequently Ernie could hardly go anywhere except where Dickie led him.

'Open the window, boy!'

Oh God, I thought, we're going to have one of Dickie's jokes! He had three jokes. This was Number Three.

Big Ernie struggled to push up the sash window. When he'd got it open about two feet Dickie suddenly grabbed him round the knees and made as if to chuck him out of the window into the street three storeys below.

'You're a useless article, boy, what are you?'

'A useless article, sir,' Ernie answered dutifully, his head half-way out of the window.

'And who wants a useless article?'

'Nobody, sir.'

'Right,' leered Dickie. 'So if nobody wants you, you might as well jump out of this window and as you float through the air, say to yourself, "Here goes nothing!" '

As he shoved Ernie a few inches further out of the window, his weasel eyes whipped round the room to make sure his audience was responding correctly.

'Ha, ha, ha!' we all chirped. 'Ha, ha ha!' Until he turned away. End of joke. The feeblest joke in the world. Except for his other two!

Then – he slammed down the window and gave Ernie an open-handed clout across the face that sent him spinning down the gangway. He followed it with a left and right to the side of Ernie's head and a short-arm thunderbolt that knocked him sprawling on the floor.

Of all the barbaric teachers I came across – and there were more than some people would have you believe – Dickie Sharpe was the only one who positively gloated over his victims. He stood, now, with the sole of his boot resting on Ernie's cheek, rolling the boy's head from side to side like some crummy Roman gladiator who'd just won a duel with a tame rabbit.

A new sadistic torture flashed into the gladiator's mind. He began to propel Ernie, by a mixture of kicks and pushes, towards the big oak cupboard by the desk. He ordered two lads in the front row to open the cupboard doors, whereupon he rolled Ernie right into the bottom of it. With his feet he forced Ernie's arms and legs into the available space – and then kicked the door shut.

In spite of the fact that breathing out loud was a punishable offence, an audible gasp ran through the class.

He'll die, I remember thinking. There's no way air can get into that solid cupboard. Big Ernie's going to suffocate. I wonder if they'll close the school for a half-day for the funeral. And I hope they hang Dickie Sharpe for murder.

When Ernie was yanked out of his solitary confinement at the end of the lesson he appeared none the worse for his torture apart from the fluff and dust he'd collected. Was I alone in being the tiniest bit disappointed there wasn't a body in the cupboard? I didn't want Ernie dead, God knows – but I did fancy Dickie Sharpe being hanged!

[138]

At playtime, Ernie ran home. I'd never known Ernie do it before. Some kids had, but I never reckoned on it – if you were found out it was a swift trip to the headmaster's office and three stripes of his swishy cane on each hand.

We had our own teacher, Miss Armitage, after break and she didn't seem to notice he was missing, so naturally none of us said a word. At quarter-past four when the bell rang for home time, I rushed out across the yard to meet my current mate, Georgie Johnson, who was in the class below mine. He was on his honour to wait for me by the long wall behind the boys' lavs because we had a game of fag-cards to finish which we'd started the night before, and he was winning. He had to give me a chance to win back my lost cards and my self-respect, so while we settled to a session of 'flicks the farthest' I told him about Big Ernie. I was just getting to the bit where he shoved him in the cupboard when Ernie himself comes trundling across the allotments. And coming up fast behind him was an even larger edition of himself which just had to be his Dad. It was obvious they were heading for the school and equally obvious who they were after. As they came through the gate into the yard, Georgie and I nipped round behind the woodwork hut and slipped into the school building through the back lobby. We hoped against hope that we might see the confrontation. And for once my hopes were more than fulfilled. Big Ernie's Dad and Dickie Sharpe came face to face in the corridor not more than ten paces away from where Georgie and I were tucked away in the corner by the sink.

'Is this 'im?' Big Ern Senior asked his offspring, jerking this thumb towards Dickie.

'That's 'im,' mumbled Ernie.

'I wants you, matey!'

'I beg your pardon.' Dickie's voice still sounded posh compared with Ernie's Dad, but it had an unfamiliar waver about it.

'Never mind beggin' me pardon, matey. Are you the one what locked our Ernie in a cupboard – an' kicked 'im – and got fluff all over 'is clean jersey what 'is mother jus' washed las' week?'

'Well, now – er – look here, Mr – er –' Dickie was really spluttering now. Georgie and me were trembling with laughter and excitement.

'Look 'ere, matey –' Ernie's Dad had a handful of the front of Dickie's jacket in his huge fist – 'I can 'it 'im an' 'is Ma can 'it 'im but if you lays 'ands on 'im agen, I'll break your so-and-so neck.'

Ernie's Dad was beginning to swear better than my Gramp – and he was pretty good when he got going.

'I shall report you –' Dickie blubbed.

'Who to?' Ernie's Dad shoved his whiskery face right into Dickie's. 'I ain't never set eyes on yer an' there ain't no witness to prove I 'ave.'

Dickie gazed round desperately but there was no witness in sight, Big Ernie having beaten a nimble retreat once his Dad started operations. 'So if you goes reportin' me to anybody, all it means is – you'll get your so-and-so neck broke a damn sight sooner!'

After a bit more cussing and a few more threats, Ernie's Dad ambled off, leaving an open-mouthed, sweating hulk of flesh leaning limply against the corridor wall.

It was some minutes before Dickie was in a fit state to stagger off home and Georgie and I crept out of our cramped hiding-place. We could hardly believe what we had seen now it was all over. The cold, empty, darkening corridor could never before have witnessed such momentous events. Could it?

[140]

We trotted home along the old canal path hugging our secret to ourselves. We didn't talk about it at all – we were both too busy having action replays inside our minds, fixing the picture so clearly in our heads that I can see it now as if it had happened only last night. Ernie's Dad towering over Dickie Sharpe, one great fist clutching the lapel of Dickie's tweed suit, the other hovering an inch away from Dickie's bulbous, purple conk . . .!

I tried to imagine the scene in the playground the next morning when Georgie and I regaled our mates with the sensational story in every fond detail. Yet when the morning came – we said nothing. It was as if we both realised that it was a story which belonged only to us – that could never be properly told or properly understood. And I knew that the ending to the story had not yet happened.

The next Thursday I couldn't keep my eyes off Dickie and Ernie. It was as if an invisible cord was keeping them apart – and yet I was sure it would draw them together before the lesson ended. There were barely five minutes left when the cord drew Dickie, in his silent, rubbersoled, shiny, black boots, along the gangway towards where Big Ernie was constructing a multi-sided parallelogram.

'That's not quite right, lad.'

Everybody thought their ears were playing tricks. Fifty pairs of eyes left their exercise books.

'You haven't quite got the idea of where to start, have you, lad?'

Dickie took the stump of blunt, chewed pencil from Ernie's fingers and tossed it into the waste basket. He took a long, thin, sharp pencil from his inside jacket pocket and drew Ernie's parallelogram for him.

When he had finished, he patted Ernie on the shoulder and walked away.

'Sir!' said Ernie, holding out the long, thin, sharp pencil.

'That's all right, lad. You keep it. There's plenty more where that one came from!'

For the first time in my life I envied Big Ernie. I envied him his Dad. Well, I mean to say, what an advantage he had over me! My Dad was about five foot eight and nine stone and a stores issuer and he wouldn't have said boo to a small goose. So what chance had I got against the Dickie Sharpes of this world!

Tar and Treasure

We sat in a row on our front garden wall. Like a line of Humpty Dumpties waiting for a fall. Except none of us was as egg-shaped as the Humpty Dumpties in the picture books. I don't remember there being so many fat kids in those days. Because we didn't eat so much, I suppose. You couldn't exactly stuff yourself on sweets, either; not when you got a penny a week pocket money. No, when we were young we all seemed to have a skinnier, paler, knobblier look than today's kids.

'I reckon it's the loveliest smell what was ever invented,' breathed Vic.

'I never gets tired of it,' added Spud.

'Nor me,' I agreed.

We sat with beatific smiles on our grubby faces, nostrils flared and eyes a-sparkle just like the Bisto Kids in the posters.

'Better 'n 'orse dung!' I added.

''Orse dung!' scoffed Vic. 'I don't see 'ow you can compare that wi' this.'

'I can,' piped up Albie. 'I likes 'orse dung smells. When it's fresh an' all 'ot an' steamin' an' –'

'Ugh!' Merv pulled a face.

''S good for the garden,' I said sounding just like my

[143]

Dad. Every time a horse dropped a little pile outside our house it was my job to nip out with shovel and bucket and claim it before old Mr Waller from number twenty-nine got there. Between the Co-op bakers' van, the GWR coal cart and Eddie Quilter's milk dray, my Dad's little square of black dirt behind the coal-bunk was liberally supplied with golden-brown doughnuts of fertiliser.

And he grew good rhubarb and pansies, and cabbage plants that he took down his allotment and planted again, more spaced out.

'I dunno 'ow you can even think of that – that – muck!' snorted Vic. 'Not when there's 'ot tar to smell.'

And I had to agree that the aroma of boiling tar being sprayed on the road took some whacking.

'All smells is diff'rent,' said Albie the peacemaker. 'It's 'ard to say what's nicest. Depends what one you're smellin' at the minute!'

'I know what one I'm smellin',' breathed Merv, his eyes closed, a heavenly smile bisecting his face.

We all sniffed appreciatively as the tar hissed and glistened on the smooth road.

'Wish I 'ad a pair o' gum boots like 'im,' sighed Spud.

We all gazed enviously at the rubber thigh boots worn by the man who actually did the spraying. Not that you could see the rubber, they were coated all over with layers of solidified tar. They would have surely stood up on their own without any legs in them!

Truly, Ol' Gus, the tar-sprayer, was a magnificent sight, from his flat cap (which he wore back to front, with the peak sticking out behind and the rim resting on his ears), his huge gauntlet gloves which almost enveloped his elbows, and his rubber apron, to his magnificent thigh boots.

Oh yes, not forgetting the goggles! A frightening pair

of eye-pieces which covered half his face when he was spraying and all of his forehead when he was resting.

He rested quite a lot. After a steady burst of spraying, swinging the nozzle of his hose-pipe back and forth from the centre of the road to the gutter as he backed away towards the steaming tar-engine which supplied the boiling black liquid, he would switch off, lay aside the hose, sit on the edge of the pavement, throw off his gauntlets, dive under his apron and produce a paper-pack of five Woodbines. He could drag a cig out of the packet no-handed by the tips of his teeth. (I used to practise on my Dad's but all I got was a soggy packet, a horrible chewed tobacco taste and a clipped ear!)

The young chap who looked after the fire in the tar-engine had a knack of anticipating when Gus would take his next break and always appeared with a glowing ember from the fire-box to light the inevitable Woodbine.

'I know what I'm gonna be when I grows up,' murmured Albie.

'An' me,' I said.

Then Vic had to go and spoil it by stating the obvious. ''Ow many tar sprayin' men d'you think there are in the world? There's only one in each town.'

'In that case,' said Merv, quietly, but taking Vic down off his high-horse, 'I'll prob'ly be the nex' one round 'ere 'cos I'm the oldest an' I'll jus' about be leavin' school when Ol' Gus retires.'

'Hey! Look out!' yelled Spud suddenly. 'It's the gritters!'

We all tumbled backwards off the wall and hid in our front garden, only our eyes and noses visible. No longer a row of Humpty Dumpties, more like a line of Mr Chads.

The gritters were the two men whose signal to begin

work was the ritual lighting of Gus's fag. They shovelled the grit from heaps which had been strategically dumped along the road long before the arrival of Gus and his mate and their horse-drawn, iron monster which spewed lovely boiling tar from its steaming bowels. With practised art they slung their shovelfuls of grit across the freshly tarred surface, spreading it neatly and evenly with smooth, controlled swings of their shovels.

Albie and me had practised it many a time down the end of our garden with my Dad's spade but we only finished up with our shoes full of dirt and mole-hill heaps of soil all over the garden path.

'It's the shape of our Dad's spade,' I consoled Albie. 'The ones what the gritters use are a speshul, slingin' sort o' shape.'

The reason for our hasty retreat behind the wall was that these two particular gritters had a playful habit of spattering the grit on the pavement so it bounced up and stung us on the legs.

'Where've them cissies gone, then, 'arold?' asked the big ginger bloke with warts sprouting on his nose like dull brown mushrooms. He shaded his eyes with his hand, pretending to search the somewhat limited landscape. It was all part of the game.

'Gone 'ome to their Mams I shouldn't wonder,' Harold replied, hurling a shovelful of grit against the wall right under our noses, sending the prickly stone chippings richochetting up into our faces. I think they really hated kids, those two.

'They'm better off there, tied to their Mam's apron strings,' chortled Ginger, spraying his next load at such an angle that it fanned out and spattered against the wall like machine-gun fire.

A chip stung Spud's cheek.

Forgetting the danger, Spud leapt to his feet.

Vic said later, ''E could've bin stoned to death. Like that saint. Stephen, I think 'e was. Saint Spud – the first Corporation martyr!'

'You big, ginger sod!' howled Spud – and he didn't swear much, Spud didn't – 'I'll get the law on you! An' me Dad!'

Ginger's ugly mug was further distorted by a fearsome grin disclosing assorted molars which matched the colour of his hair. He leaned on his shovel and gobbed into the pile of grit.

'Fetch'n out, then, an' let's see 'ow 'e matches up,' scoffed Ginger, flexing one huge bicep under his rolled shirt sleeve.

Then Vic joined the fray. You could always bank on Vic to come up with a corking bit of back-chat when it was most needed. 'You wanna watch it, Ginger,' he yelled from behind the wall. 'It's gettin' excited as makes them warts grow. You'll soon 'ave more warts than what you've got nose!'

'Yer cheeky young swine,' shrieked Ginger, falling off his shovel.

Vic had gone too far this time. An immediate show of cowardice was called for. We were over the wall in two shakes of a lamb's tail and you couldn't see our heels for loose chippings as we tore off down the street.

'You'll 'ave worse'n warts if I catches you a fourpenny one with this shovel,' we heard Ginger's throaty cry from a long way off.

His mate was shouting things, too, but we were in no mood to stop and listen.

'Did you 'ear that?' panted Spud as we scooted round the corner into the backs behind Vic's house.

''Ear what?'

'Ol' Gus. The tar-sprayin' man.'

'I know 'e's the tar-sprayin' man! What about 'im?'

''E spoke!'

''E never did!'

''E did, too. I 'eard 'im.'

'What did 'e say, then?'

Spud held back till we were near busting with suspense.

''E said,' Spud announced. ''E said, "Good on yer, laddie. That's took 'im down a peg or two!" '

'Blimey!' breathed Albie. 'Fancy Ol' Gus ackchully speakin'. To us!'

'To me!' Spud puffed out his chest.

'It don't matter 'oo to, do it?' said Merv. ''E spoke. An' that's the firs' time I knew 'e could talk!'

'You wants yer 'ead read,' sneered Vic. 'Di'n't think 'e could talk! D'you think 'is tongue's all stuck up wi' tar or summat?'

'I only said I'd never 'eard 'im,' countered Merv. 'I only said –'

'I only said!' mimicked Vic. ''Ow d'you think 'e asks 'is mate to make up the fire, or asks at the shop for 'is Woodies, or asks –'

''E could've been struck dumb,' Albie suggested.

'Dumb! Oh crikey!' Vic howled. ''Ow daft can you get? D'you think –'

'Never mind all that,' I chipped in before they started scrapping. 'What we gonna do now? We can't go back an' watch 'em sprayin' no more today.'

'Nor a few more days, neither,' added Spud. 'Not till they've forgot about it.'

'I shouldn't think Ginger'll ever forget,' said Merv sadly. 'People never get over it if you says things about their face. I said our Gran 'ad a better moustache than what Groucho Marx 'ad an' she've never got over it! Two years ago, an' I ain't never 'ad a birthday present nor a Christmas present ever since!'

[148]

'Never mind about 'er,' I exploded. 'What about us? I mean, what we gonna do for the rest o' the mornin'?'

'I know,' said Albie quietly. 'We'll play Corporation workmen ourselves! We ain't done no diggin' for ages.'

We considered Albie's proposition.

'Whose garden we gonna do it in?'

'Not ours,' said Merv and Spud and Vic almost exactly together.

'An' it can't be mine,' I apologised. 'My Dad said 'e'd flay me alive if we dug up our garden again. 'E says 'is broad beans an' cabbages won't stand bein' dug up an' put back any more!'

'It'll 'ave to be yours, then, Albie,' said Vic.

'I dunno,' Albie began.

'Well, we ain't done no pipe layin' in your garden for a good while,' Merv pointed out.

So we voted four to one in favour of playing navvies in Albie's bit of back garden. The gardens of our little two-up, two-down and a scullery-stuck-on-the-back terraced houses were somewhat smaller than the proverbial pocket handkerchief. And when you allowed for the shed, the coal-bunker and the outside lavvy, the actual acreage of dirt for growing things was about twelve square yards. Most of our Dads grew a row of sweet peas along the dividing fence, a row of pansies along the edge of the red brick path, and devoted the rest to a few veg or used it for starting off cabbage plants and the like ready for transplanting down the allotment at the right time.

Albie's Dad was one of the allotment brigade. I was afraid we wouldn't find much room for digging in his sacred plot. But when we inspected it, we found a patch of virgin black dirt about six feet square, between the pansies and the sweet peas.

'That'll do,' said Vic.

'But 'e might 'ave seeds in,' Albie protested.

'Ain't no seeds in there,' announced Vic, with the sort of authoritative tone of a juvenile Mr Middleton, the chap who talked about gardening to all our Dads on the wireless. 'Too late for seeds. They goes in in the spring.'

'But 'e might 'ave some late sproutin' brocc'li in there,' Albie pleaded. 'Well, I mean, I've 'eard of early sproutin' stuff so I 'spec' there's late sproutin' stuff as well!'

'Ain't nothin' 'ere.' Vic stirred the lifeless, coal-black dirt with his heel. No wonder my Dad sent me scurrying off for horse dung to put some body back into the soil. It had been growing the same old things over and over for close on fifty years. It looked properly worn out. In Albie's garden just like in ours.

''Ow many spades you got?' Merv enquired.

We searched Albie's shed and came up with one proper garden spade with a broken shaft, a rusty coal shovel and Albie's little sister's tin seaside spade.

''S not much use,' moaned Vic.

'I could nip 'ome an' get our Dad's fork,' Spud offered.

''Ow you gonna get 'ome without passin' Ginger? You'll 'ave to go via the Isle o' Wight if you don't want 'im to see you,' Vic said sarcastically.

'Let's make do wi' what we got,' I said. 'We can 'ave three diggin' an' one gettin' the pipes ready what we're gonna lay an' one –' I paused a moment, then concluded brilliantly – 'an' one foreman!'

'An' who's that goin' to be?' demanded Vic, hoping his size and tone of voice would together intimidate me into offering him the job.

'Albie,' I said bravely. 'It's 'is garden.'

Even Vic couldn't deny that.

[150]

'Tha's right,' agreed Merv. 'Albie ought to be in charge. Well, I mean, it'll be 'im as gets belted if 'is Dad catches us, won't it?'

Albie, who had been somewhat cheered by the prospect of the position of foreman, now resumed his former expression of misery.

'Go careful, Vic,' he pleaded desperately. 'Don't tread on nothin'. An' don't pile the earth on the path. An' be careful with our Ivy's spade or our Mam'll clout me. An' don't lean on the fence 'cos it's a bit weak. An' let's 'urry up an' get it finished before our Mam gets 'ome. She've only gone down the Chinese laundry with our Dad's Sunday collars!'

'Cor, blimey!' Spud said admiringly. ''E's a nachral foreman, ain't 'e? Nothin' but moanin', jus' like the one our Dad's always cussin' about!'

We set to work to dig a hole deep enough to lay pipes. Gas? Electric? Drainage? Sewers? I don't know. We never thought about that. Just a nice trench, about five feet by two and deep enough so that the sides wouldn't cave in even though we got well down into the gooey, yellow clay. And then some freshly chopped sticks of firewood laid lovingly end to end in the bottom of the trench. Like the pipes that the workmen laid when they dug up the road.

''Urry up!' Albie clasped his hands in front of his chest like the local vicar did when he requested us to stop kicking our football up against the vestry wall during choir practice. 'Don't bother 'bout goin' as deep as usual.'

'Gotta do it proper,' said Vic malevolently. 'Gotta get down to the clay.'

'I 'ave!' Merv announced, bringing up a dollop of the stuff. It was just like the plasticine we used to have in Miss Price's class in Queenstown Infants'.

'Make sure the yellow all goes back in the bottom,' Albie pleaded, hopping about from one foot to the other as if he was a fire dancer. 'If any of it gets left on top our Dad'll know an' 'e'll –'

Albie's voice spluttered and packed up, unable to find words to express what tortures his Dad might perpetrate on him if he discovered his garden tampered with.

'I think I've struck somethin'!'

Spud straightened up, one hand clutching the small of his back in real professional digging style.

'You've bent it!' wailed Albie. 'You've gone an' bent it!'

'I couldn't 'elp it, could I? Not if I struck somethin'. I mean to say –'

Albie snatched his sister's toy spade from Spud's hands and began frantically trying to straighten the pathetically twisted tin blade by squashing it against the path with his foot.

'Our Ivy'll find out for sure,' Albie cried, his efforts to straighten the thin metal only resulting in a sort of S-shaped blade. 'An' she'll tell our Mam.' The tears began to wash clean patches on his cheeks. 'An' she'll go an' tell our Dad.' The tears became a veritable waterfall.

'Don't worry,' I patted Albie's shoulder. 'We'll buy 'er a new un.'

Albie checked a sob. 'What with?' he enquired hopelessly.

'I dunno,' I admitted. 'But we will. Some 'ow. Won't we, Spud?'

Spud nodded. Well I mean, it was him that did it, not me. I don't know why I should be promising reparation. Except that Albie was my best mate. And he would have expected it of me.

'It cost,' Albie blubbed, 'it cost – sixpence!'

Oh heck! Sixpence. Six weeks of Friday pennies.

Nearly two month's savings. Unless everybody dibbed in a bit.

'On the beach.'

'Do what, Albie?'

'On the beach. That's where 'er spade come from. The stall neares' the pier at Weston. The one with the tables an' benches outside where you gets the jugs o' tea an' 'ot pies.'

'Jus' what the doctor ordered,' boomed a strange voice from over the yard wall. 'A jug o' tea an' an 'ot pie.'

'Oh Dad!' Albie wailed and hurled himself into his father's brawny arms. 'I've gone an' bent our Ivy's new spade.'

There's loyalty for you, I thought. Not, 'Spud's gone an' bent it.' Taking the blame on himself. And there's low cunning for you, too, I thought. Getting in first before they get a chance to biff you one.

'I never meant to, Dad. It was an accident. I mean, well, it couldn't 'ave been very strong. Spud only – I mean, I only jus' 'ad a little dig an' –'

I had the feeling Albie's Dad wasn't listening. When I dared to look into his face I met a look of utter disbelief. Not about the spade. I knew where he was looking. Albie suddenly sensed it, too.

'It's not a very big 'ole, Dad. Not reelly. Not 'alf as deep as the one we dug in Merv's garden. An' we was jus' goin' to fill it all in nice an' smooth afore you come 'ome an' then there was this accident with the spade. I don't reckon it was worth sixpence, Dad. Shall we ask 'im for our money back when we goes to Weston nex' year?'

'Where d'you get it from?' boomed Albie's Dad.

'We got it off the stall by the pier –'

'Not that!' Albert senior thrust Albert junior aside and advanced belligerently on the near-paralytic Spud.

'I di'n't mean to, Mr Cullin'ford. I was diggin' ever so gently an' –'

[153]

'Where d'you get that box?'

I thought the conversation was all about holes and spades. What was he on about boxes for?

'What box, Mr Cullin'ford?' Vic was also obviously puzzled.

By way of answer, Albie's Dad almost fell into our hole in his enthusiasm to get at the red and dirt-coloured object at Spud's feet which he apparently recognised as a box. He began to clean it up on the sleeve of his boiler suit.

'I don' b'lieve it,' he muttered to himself, oblivious of holes in gardens and bent spades. Oblivious even of the five guilt-ridden figures clustered like five miniature grave-diggers around a miniature grave. ''Ow the 'eck did it get there?'

It was a rhetorical question which no one answered because nobody knew what he was on about.

Leastways, four of us didn't. Albie's face took on a sort of half-knowing look.

'Ain't that your Diddle'um box, Dad?'

Mr Cullingford turned slowly towards his eldest offspring. His eyes narrowed – just like James Cagney. His lip curled – just like Humphrey Bogart. His jaw jutted – just like Edward G. Robinson.

'An' what do you know about this, then, Long John Silver? Where d'you find the map o' the 'idden treasure? Eh?'

Albie backed off towards the coalbunk.

'I di'n't put it there, Dad. They'll tell you. I di'n't even want to dig in our garden. Did I?' Light suddenly dawned as though a switch had been thrown in his brain. 'Our Ivy! It must 'ave been our Ivy what buried it. She's always 'idin' things.'

'That's when the spade got bent!' Spud was quick to spot a chance of unloading his own guilt. 'It mus' 'ave bin bent already an' I never noticed. Well, I mean, you don't always look to see if you got a bent spade!'

But no one was listening. All eyes were on the box as Albie's Dad lifted it to his ear and rattled it. It sounded pretty full to me.

'There's a lot o' money in there, by the sound of it, Mr Cullin'ford,' said Vic.

'Aye,' said Albie's Dad. 'There's some silver an' copper in there, lad. Near on ten pounds worth, I reckon.' He lifted the box up on eye level and shook some more. 'That's if the lock 'aven't been messed about with.'

He inspected the tiny key-hole and scraped away some more dirt. 'Not thinkin' o' runnin' off with the proceeds, Mister Sec'tary, eh?'

Albie's Dad leaped as if stung by a bee. But if he was surprised by the voice over the garden wall it was nothing to the effect it had on us five kids. We were round the back of the shed like a flash from a gun. It wasn't only the voice, it was the face that went with it. That great bush of ginger hair. And all those warts.

''Ello, Cecil,' said Albert's Dad meekly.

Cecil! A Cecil with ginger hair and warts and great muscles like a Mr Atlas? Fred, perhaps, or 'Arry, or Reg, or George, or Alf – but not Cecil, surely!

'Don't tell me you keeps it buried in the garden, Albert,' Cecil guffawed. 'Mus' be a bit of a bother diggin' it up ev'ry time somebody pays up 'is dues.'

Mr Cullingford stared into the hole as if he had noticed it for the first time.

'Them kids,' he breathed. 'It's them blasted kids, Cecil.'

I peered round the corner of the shed. Cecil stood, his brawny fore-arms folded along the yard wall, his mind slowly putting two and two together and getting very close to four.

[155]

'Kids,' he echoed Albie's Dad, 'there was some kids dodged off round the back o' your shed jus' when I got 'ere, Albert. An' you know what? I reckons as 'ow they might be the same little swine as been back-chattin' me down the street not so long back.'

For a moment I thought Albie's Dad was going to rout us out from our hiding-place so that he and Cecil could clout our ears from one end of the yard to the other for all the morning's misdemeanours – holes, boxes, spades, warts. The lot!

Then Cecil said, 'I 'ope as 'ow it weren't one o' your lads as called out at me. 'Cos 'ooever 'e might be, I'll like as not murder the little so-an'-so if I lays 'ands on 'im.'

Mr Cullingford hesitated. Then, deciding that Cecil meant business and he didn't really want to see Albie slain on his own garden path, he turned towards the scullery door.

'Never mind the kids, Cecil. Come on in an' 'ave a drop o' dandelion wine. I jus' opened 'im las' night an' 'e's beautiful. One o' last year's, 'e is.'

As the two men moved away towards the house Cecil was still on about the box.

'I still don't see what you was doin' down the garden with the box. I mean, it's all covered wi' dirt. You weren't really –'

The dark green door closed, the latch clicked down and we all breathed out for the first time in what seemed like hours.

'The myst'ry o' the red tin box.' Spud broke our long silence.

'I don't get it.' Vic pinched his nose between finger and thumb which he always did when he couldn't quite figure things out.

'What don't you get?' asked Albie innocently.

[156]

''Undreds o' things,' Merv chipped in. 'Your Dad knowin' ol' Ginger Wart-face for a start.'

'You mean Cecil,' I said in a posh voice, and we all rolled about on the floor laughing.

'Yeah, fancy 'im knowin' Cecil,' Vic persisted when he had recovered a bit.

'Well, why not?' countered Albie. 'I 'spect 'e knew 'im in the army. My Dad knew a lot o' blokes when 'e was in the war. In the Wilts Yeomanry, my Dad was, an' 'e went to India an' Egg-wiped an' France –'

'Where's Egg-wiped?' asked Merv.

'Egypt,' Vic told him. 'It's one of Albie's Dad's old jokes.'

'My Dad went all over,' Albie said hotly. 'Mes'pota-mia an' Belgium an' the Isle o' Man –'

'Yeah, we know all that, we've 'eard it about an 'undred times before.' Spud interrupted Albie's flow, like he alway did, because his Dad wasn't in the war and it made him feel different from the rest of us because all our Dads were in it.

'What I didn't get,' said Vic, giving his nose another tug, 'was that stuff about diddlin' 'em.'

'You mean – the Diddle'um box?' Albie looked incredulous. 'You ain't never 'eard of a Diddle'um box?'

'Never.'

We all shook our heads.

'You mean – none o' your Dads pays in a Diddle'um club?'

Albie stared at our blank faces in total disbelief, as if we had just denied that Arsenal were the greatest football team in the world.

'Well, I don't know 'ow you manages for Christmas,' he said despairingly.

'Our Mum 'as Provvy cheques,' Merv suggested hopefully.

'Ev'rybody 'as them,' sneered Vic. 'You wouldn't never get no new clothes without Provvy cheques, would you? Stands to reason, nobody can pay two or three pounds for suits an' dresses an' shoes an' things with money.'

'Never mind all that.' I was dying to know about this diddle'um thing. 'What about this club o' your Dad's, Albie?'

''E runs two ev'ry year,' Albie explained. We gathered round him, eyes goggling, ears flapping. 'One starts at the beginnin' o' the year an' pays for their day at the races in the summer an' then, soon as that one's over, they starts payin' in again for Christmas.'

'Who pays?' asked Spud.

'The blokes down the workin' men's club.'

'But what's the diddle 'em bit?'

Albie, enjoying lording it over the rest of us for once, savoured the moment before replying.

'Well, 's like this,' he said eventually, like a teacher instructing a class of half-baked dim-wits. 'You starts off by payin' a ha'penny the first week. An' then you pays a penny nex' week. An' tuppence the next. An' you goes on doublin' up ev'ry week.'

He beamed at us. Then Merv chopped him down to size.

'Well, if that's all it is, I don't reckon much to it. An' I can't see as 'ow you'd 'ave much of a Christmas, jus' puttin' in ha'pennies an' pennies.'

'Aha!' crowed Albie. 'An' that's where you'd be wrong, Mervyn Know-all. If you was any good at 'rithmetic you'd know that keepin' on doublin' up you'd be payin' in – well, pounds an' pounds by the end. Las' year we 'ad chicken an' a whackin' great 'am an' enough bottles o' beer to fill all the space between the sofa an' the wall in our front room! All out o' the Diddle'um Club.'

[158]

We marvelled at the ingenuity of Albie's Dad.

A sudden thought spoiled the moment. 'Albie,' I asked, 'why does 'e call it a Diddle'um Club?'

Albie's moon face clouded over.

'Yeah,' chimed in Vic. 'It sounds sort o' funny to me. 'Oo was diddlin' 'oo, Albie?'

Albie's fists came up instinctively in defence of his father.

'My Dad di'n't diddle nobody,' he spat at Vic, tight-lipped, his cheeks flushed scarlet. 'I don't know why they call 'em that. But they do. My Auntie Vi runs one down at 'er sewin' circle. An' if you says anythin' else 'bout my Dad –'

He left the sentence unfinished. But the threat was enough for Vic who, though half a head taller than Albie, recognised danger when he smelt it and backed off.

'Don't go gettin' mad,' he whined. 'I only meant –'

Whatever he meant we never knew because at that moment Albie's Dad came out of the house followed by *his* friend Cecil, *our* enemy, Ginger Wart-face. They both had that glazed, contented look that my Dad used to get after a touch of the dandelion wine.

It was too late to run. We just stood like five statues waiting for Cecil to recognise us and hurl himself upon us.

But he only grinned at us. For one awful second I thought he was gong to smash Merv's skull with his huge fist. Then he patted him on the head.

''Ere,' Albie's Dad turned at the back-gate, his hand in his trousers back pocket, 'I s'pose you're entitled to some sort o' reward for discov'rin' the buried treasure.' He considered the coin in his palm for so long I was afraid he would have second thoughts and put it back.

''Ere,' he said at long last, 'an' don't forget what a good father you got.'

[159]

He flicked the silver threepenny bit high in the air and Albie caught it expertly.

Cecil, who had been watching over the garden wall, suddenly looked at Vic with a new and ugly expression. You could almost hear his brain ticking over as it struggled to focus.

'C'mon, Cecil,' called Albie's Dad, already half-way down the backway. 'Hi, Albie, tell your mother I've gone up the club an' to put me dinner in the oven. C'mon, Cecil, they'll be closed 'fore we gets there.'

There was a pause about half the length of eternity before Cecil turned and lumbered away after Mr Cullingford. You could have heard our sighs of relief all the way down the street. We gathered silently around the little open grave which had so recently disgorged its treasure.

Eventually, Spud chirped up.

'We gonna finish it, then?'

'Eh?'

'The game. We gonna finish layin' the pipes?'

The rest of us had lost interest in pipe-laying.

'What about spendin' that threepenny joey then, Albie?' said Vic. Trust him!

Albie hesitated.

'Well, I mean, it ain't yours, 'xactly, is it?' persisted Vic. 'I mean, 'e gave it you 'cos 'e's your ole chap but 'e must 'ave meant it for all of us 'cos we all 'elped to find it, di'n't we?'

'Well, 'f it comes to that,' Spud chipped in, 'I should think it's mine. It was me what dug it up – ackchully dug it up – wasn't it?'

Albie turned on Spud like a magistrate about to pass sentence. ''F it comes to that, Spud Taylor, you owes me sixpence for breakin' our Ivy's spade. So if I gives you the joey for ackchully findin' the box –' at this point he solemnly placed the coin in Spud's hand – 'an' then you gives it back to me to 'elp buy our Ivy a new spade –' he equally solemnly took the coin back again – 'then we'll be quits!'

I gazed at Albie with great admiration. It was such a logical, fair way to handle the matter. Even if Vic did look as though he'd been done out of his share of a small fortune.

''Ere,' I said, ''ave you lot thought o' summat? If ol' Ginger Cecil 'ave gone off boozin' with Albie's Dad, they'll sure to be gone for ages. So there ain't nothin' to stop us goin' back an' watchin' ol' Gus spraying'. I bet 'e've started again by now.'

I could see they all had the same vision. Hot tar gushing out of Gus's nozzle, gleaming shiny black on the road, the steam drifting into our eager nostrils –

It was a race to see who could get there first, me and Albie leading Merv and Spud by what my Gramp would have called a gnat's whisker. Vic was sort of left at the post. When he caught us up he had a funny look on his face, like somebody who had been double-crossed and still couldn't believe his rotten luck.

We sat in a row on the kerb watching, breathless, as Gus adjusted his goggles and his gauntlets and prepared to put on a matinee performance for his eager audience.

''Bout that threepenny joey,' Vic began.

''E's goin' to switch on,' breathed Merv.

'I reckon your Dad meant –' Vic tried again.

'Any minute now,' sighed Spud.

'An' I tell you summat else,' Vic persisted, ''bout this club thing. This diddle'um. I don't understand –'

'Shurrup, Vic,' said Albie.

Gus switched on. The hot tar sizzled and sparkled in the sunshine. Black, liquid gold.

My Uncle George

I had a heck of a collection of uncles. My Dad's brothers. My Mum's brothers. Their brothers-in-law and cousins. And a lot who weren't real uncles but worked with my Dad in the railway sheds or went to school with him or were neighbours. Pretty well every grown-up man who came to our house was called uncle.

Uncle George was the best. Easily. In fact, once you started thinking about Uncle George, no one else rated at all.

He was a real uncle. My Dad's youngest brother. He looked like a half-size model of my Dad. Same grey eyes, hollow cheeks, bony jaw. Same sort of short-back-and-sides haircut, stooped shoulders, Burton's three-guinea Sunday suit.

The only difference was, he looked ten years older than my Dad although he was actually a good few years younger.

'It was Wipers as done for our George,' my father always used to say.

'Well, at least he's still with us which is more'n can be said for my brother Alf,' my mother would reply, never looking up from her darning.

'Oh aye, 'e's still with us! What's left of 'im, that is.'

'What 'appened to him at Wipers?' I asked. I knew well enough, but I had to keep hearing it. I had nightmares trying to picture it, my little Uncle George and an enormous German soldier charging one another with fixed bayonets on the battlefield at Ypres.

''E got a bayonet in 'is guts, that's what. Left for dead, 'e was. With a great 'ole in 'is belly an' 'is life-blood drainin' away. It's a miracle 'e's 'ere at all.'

'Well, let's be thankful for the miracle, then,' said my Mum, squirming at the horror of it all, while I tried desperately to conjure up the scene and prepare myself for another nightmare.

'Left all night in no-man's-land, 'e was,' my father went on, better able to imagine it all than me because he'd been in the war, too, though he came out of it all right except for being gassed, which made him cough a lot in the winter. 'Lyin' there in the mud an' rain till this stretcher bearer noticed 'im twitchin' an' they crawled out o' their trench an' dragged 'im back.'

My Uncle George was five foot six and about seven stone and looked as if a puff of wind would shift him clean off his feet.

'Smart little feller 'e were before 'e joined the Light Infantry, weren't 'e, mother? Sixteen, 'e was. Put 'is age on so's 'e could join up. Silly young beggar.'

But I knew my Dad was very proud of him. I found out years later that it was my Dad that spoke to the foreman and got George put on light work when his stomach was playing him up so bad he couldn't stand straight. He was a boiler-maker, George was, one of the best trades in the railway workshops, but it was heavy, tiring work even for strapping big men. For George, every nine-hour day must have been hell. But what with the short time and unemployment, he couldn't afford to pack it in. So my Dad spoke up for him and the rest of his gang used to carry him when he was having one of his bad spells.

On Friday nights, Uncle George always called for my father and they went to The Glue Pot for a couple of pints. Only a couple and only on Fridays. They couldn't afford to go out more than once a week.

Uncle George always arrived smack on eight o' clock and talked to my mother for twenty minutes while Dad was out in the scullery finishing off shaving and changing his vest and his long, woolly pants.

''Ello, Uncle George,' I would greet him. I was always waiting, half-way along the front passage, ready to let him in as soon as he gave his own special knock.

''Ello, young 'un,' he said, always cheerful, always the same, in spite of the pain and the hole in his stomach under his Burton's waistcoat. 'You bin a good lad to your Ma this week, 'ave you?'

'I fetched the coal in twice an' I got me Dad's med'cine from the surgery an' I've 'ad me 'air cut –'

'You 'ad the cane at school this week? 'Old yer 'ands out.'

He inspected my palms for the tell-tale red weals.

'Good lad. Washed be'ind yer ears?'

I turned round. He peered behind each ear, then kissed me on top of the head. He was the only person, except my Auntie Ethel, that I never backed away from when there was any kissing in the offing.

'Yer a good 'un,' he'd say. And slip a ha'penny into my hand.

It was a sort of bond between us, this Friday ha'penny. It wasn't exactly a fortune but it was money – something that neither of us had much of. He had four kids of his own and even ha'pennies counted when there were six to be fed and less than three pounds a week to do it on. Nobody knew about the Friday ha'penny – only Uncle George and me.

'Can I fill yer pipe?' I asked when he had settled in my father's arm-chair.

'Don't go tampin' it down too 'ard, then,' he said, holding out his pouch and his best briar.

I sat on the little stool in the corner of the hearth and undid the two poppers on the flap of the soft, leather pouch. The warm, cloying scent of St Bruno rose to satisfy my eager nostrils. I buried my nose deep in the pouch, nearly suffocating myself.

'You're supposed to smoke it – not eat it!' Uncle George said.

I took a wad of the warm, flaky tobacco between my finger and thumb and began to pack the blackened bowl of the pipe.

'Best pipe o' the week, I reckon,' he said, lighting it with a twirl of newspaper that he tore off the *Daily Herald* and lit by poking it between the bars of the grate. 'Yer a good pipe-filler, young 'un. Now jus' get yer 'ead out o' me pouch an' give it us back!'

When Uncle George and my Dad left for The Glue Pot I always walked as far as the railway station with them.

'Off you go, then,' my Dad would say. 'Straight 'ome an' no larkin' about.'

'An' be careful crossin' over,' added Uncle George. 'Watch out for them big lorries.'

''Night, Dad. 'Night, Uncle George.'

''Night, night, sleep tight, watch the fleas don't bite,' sang out Uncle George. 'See you nex' Friday, then.'

And I would hare off down Manchester Road to Bulgarelli's fish and chip shop and get a ha'penny-worth of scrumps and they'd last me all the way home.

Then there came this particular Sunday morning that

I'll never forget. It was in the winter of '38–'39; it might have been January, I remember the frost on the roofs and the dew-drop on my nose. My Dad was poorly with his cough and I had to go to the allotment and pick a bagful of brussels sprouts and cut the biggest two winter cabbages I could find – enough greenstuff to see the family through the week.

Our allotment was about a mile from our house, along the canal tow-path, across the other side of the town near the railway sidings. It was a big allotment, about twenty lug, and in the spring we'd often spend all day there on a Saturday. Mum and Dad and all the kids and a great basket of jam sandwiches, a thermos of tea and a bottle of Tizer. We all had jobs to do – Dad digging, Mum putting in the peas and beans and cabbage plants, and us kids hoeing and weeding and fetching cans of water from the brook when we weren't watching the trains go by. I hated it. It put me off gardening for life.

In the winter I often had to go down the 'lottie and fetch the week's supply, Dad being poorly with his cough and Mum washing and cooking and me being the eldest and the only one with a bike. Ignoring the notice, CYCLING PROHIBITED ON THE CANAL PATH, I'd belt along on my drop-handlebar skid-iron, pick sprouts and kale and broccoli and cabbage till there was no feeling left in my bloodless, frozen fingers and then pedal laboriously back home with a bulging bag swinging from each handlebar and a heavy saddle-bag behind.

On this particular Sunday I came skidding down the cinder track that led to the ramshackle assortment of allotments, propped my bike against the fence and trotted along the crisp, grass path that divided our strip of ground from Mr Pinnock's.

I started right off picking sprouts – frozen, green

[166]

ping-pong balls that came away from the main stem with a snap – dropping them by the handful into the wide-mouthed wicker bag. Then I noticed our shed door was ajar. Fearing the absolute worst, I left my job and made for the shed. It was one of the best sheds I'd ever seen, made out of railway sleepers, thickly tarred, with a corrugated iron roof and a good door that had once been the front door on somebody's house. Inside were all my Dad's tools – spade, fork, rake, hoe, dibber, watering can – and a hundred other more or less useful bits and pieces. It was always locked. My Dad never forgot. He couldn't afford to. If he'd ever had his tools nicked – well, I suppose we'd have starved to death! I could hardly bring myself to look inside. I pushed the door gingerly as if I expected King Kong himself to leap out on me. Uncle George was sitting there on my Gran's old tin trunk that was full of soot which we used for killing slugs. He sat there looking straight at me and not seeing me at all. He looked smaller than ever, his head sunk into his woolly muffler and his flat cap down almost to his eyebrows.

''Ello, Uncle George.' I offered him my usual greeting, as if I always met him in our allotment shed at nine o'clock on Sunday mornings. I tried to think of something cheerful to say. 'Reckon them sprouts 'll take a main lot o' thawin' out. Like pickin' icicles, it is.'

He seemed to notice me quite suddenly, as if I'd sprung up out of the ground. ''Ello, young 'un,' he said, and in a funny sort of flat voice he added (so he must have heard what I said) – 'They've no flavour without the frost in 'em. Never pick a sprout till she've got three good frosts inside of 'er.'

'That's what me Dad says.'

'Your Dad's always right. 'Ow's 'is cough?'

'Pretty bad. 'E was up 'alf the night.'

'It's a proper shame 'ow 'e suffers,' said Uncle George, but by the pain showing through his sad, grey eyes I knew he was suffering more.

We looked at each other for a bit, then he patted the tin trunk by his side. ''Ere, come an' sit down.' He reached into his deep coat pocket. 'Fill us a pipe.'

Soon we were both of us swathed in a cloud of warm, soothing, St Bruno smoke.

''Ow d'you get in, Uncle George?' I asked, unable to control my curiosity any longer.

'Well, I didn't pick the lock.' He looked surprised. 'Didn't you know I 'ad a key? I've allus 'ad a key, case your Dad was ever too poorly to get down 'ere, I could do a bit o'diggin' for 'im.'

Just like Uncle George – always caring about other people. Specially my Dad.

I had to ask him the obvious question. 'What you doin' down 'ere, Uncle George?'

He sucked hard on his pipe, belching out fresh clouds of smoke, and I quite thought he had not heard my question.

Then – 'I don't suppose you know what it's like not to sleep o' nights, do you, young 'un?' – and before I could answer he went on – 'I'm sure I never did at your age. Slept like a top, I did.'

'Don't you sleep nights, Uncle George?'

'On an' off, like. On an' off.'

'Di'n't you sleep las' night?'

'More off than on, I reckon.'

He took his pipe out of his mouth and gave me a little smile. Not his usual sort of curved smile that came from deep inside and lit up his whole face – just a thin, straight, artificial smile without an ounce of warmth in it.

'Is it – is it –' (I had to know!) 'is it because of – you know – Wipers?'

[168]

'Eh?'

'The war – I mean, bein' wounded an' that.'

'Oh that!' he said as if we'd discussed it a million times, though in fact I'd never mentioned it before. 'I s'pose it's to do with that in a way. It'd been all right if I'd been a pen-pusher, but bein' a boilermaker – it's been 'ard, some days – very 'ard.'

'My Dad've spoke to Mr Bullock,' I said.

'Your Dad've been real good to me, young 'un, I know it. Mr Bullock've put me on light work when 'e could, but –' his voice tailed off and he bit hard on the stem of his pipe.

'You could get a pension for war wounds,' I suggested brightly.

'I got one. Seven shillin' a week.'

'Me Mum says you ought to give up workin' inside.'

'I am givin' up!' He said it in that odd, flat tone again. 'Nex' Friday.'

I felt sick in the pit of my stomach and it was nothing to do with the St Bruno or the fact that I'd had no breakfast. For three years and more I'd seen my mother fretting herself silly on a Friday afternoon when the factory hooter boomed out and she had twenty minutes to live through while my father walked home and then we'd know whether it was going to be the dole queue or he'd be safe for another week.

'You got the sack, Uncle George?' I asked, praying it couldn't be true and knowing it was.

'Ay, young 'un. I s'pose it 'ad to come.'

Had to come! To my Uncle George, who had put his age on for his king and country and had a bayonet through his guts at sixteen and been dragged back from the brink of death through the mud and blood of Wipers?

'You're the firs' one I've told,' he said, and I was so proud my eyes overflowed.

''Aven't you told Auntie Doll?'

'That's why I 'ad to get up an' go out for a walk. I couldn't lay there alongside 'er no longer, 'er sleepin' an' knowin' nowt, an' me wide awake an' not knowin' 'ow to tell 'er.'

'But you'll 'ave to tell 'er. She'll understand. My Mum would.'

'She ain't like yer Mum, Auntie Dollie ain't. She don't like doin' without. She likes a bit o' money in 'er purse.'

I remembered things I'd heard my Mum and Dad say when I was supposed to be playing with my clockwork train set: *That woman fancies 'erself a bit,* and *She ought to spend a bit more on food an' a bit less on perms,* and, *Our George ought to've wed a woman like you, Mother, an' 'ad a bit o' nursin' an' a bit o' lovin'.*

'You won't be out o' work long, Uncle George. They're takin' on men over the quarries.'

I could have bitten my tongue off the instant I said it. Fifty hours a week quarrying would have been even more crippling than fifty hours boiler-making. The only jobs available were for strapping great blokes with hairy chests and tattooed arms and muscles everywhere. There weren't any sitting-down jobs going – and if ever a man needed a sitting-down job it was my Uncle George.

He must have picked up my thoughts. (We were always on the same wave-length, Uncle George and me. We had a gallon of the same sort of blood inside of us.)

'You make sure you work 'ard at your school lessons young 'un. Get yourself a fancy job, clerkin' or summat. You 'arkin' to me?'

'Yes, Uncle George,' I mumbled.

'No dodgin' off from school like I done, remember. You got brains. Use 'em.'

'But you 'ad to go in the war –'

'Never mind that. You won't 'ave no wars to worry

about. You jus' make the most of your opportunities. When's the scholarship exam?'

'Feb'uary,' I said, glumly.

'You make sure you passes an' goes to the second'ry school, then. Right?'

'Right, Uncle George.'

'I bes' be gettin' along.' He eased himself off the tin trunk, doused his pipe with the ball of his thumb and pulled his muffler up round his ears.

'Shall I come up your 'ouse with you?' He looked so pitifully shrunken standing there in the shed doorway. 'I'll 'elp you tell Auntie Doll.'

'I can do me own dirty work, young 'un,' he said, without turning round. 'You get on an' pick your greens, else your Ma'll think you've got lost.'

He shuffled off along the path. When he got to the patch where the brussels sprouts were growing, he bent down and picked one out of my bag, weighed it in his hand, then wheeled round and chucked it at me.

He grinned. The old Uncle George.

'Be good,' he hollered. 'An' think on what I said.'

I stood there, numb with the cold and the sadness of it all, a greater sadness than I had ever known in my twelve years. I watched him go until his skinny, stoop-shouldered frame disappeared over the canal bridge.

He didn't call for my Dad to go to The Glue Pot the next Friday – nor the next. My father went to his house several times – a thing he had never done before – and each time he came home he looked tired and upset and said nothing.

One Saturday night in March, there was a banging on our front door and a great commotion – enough to wake me but not enough to keep me awake for long. When I got up in the morning my Dad wasn't about and

I guessed he must have had a poorly night and was lying-in. Then there were footsteps in our yard – and I would have said they were my Dad's but they were so dragging and painfully slow – and my mother opened the door and it was my Dad. He hadn't shaved and his wispy hair was blown in all directions and he wasn't wearing a tie which was very unlike my father on Sunday.

'Is it – all over?' my mother said very gently.

'Aye. Seven o'clock. Just while St Mark's church bell began soundin' for early service. Very peaceful it was.'

We all cried for a while. Then my father got very angry and started carrying on about the way the country forgot about the men who fought the war, and how a bayonet in the guts at Wipers could kill a man of a broken heart over twenty years later. Then he calmed down and began to fish in his waistcoat pockets.

''Ere,' he said, 'I dunno why but 'e said to give you this ha'penny. 'E said 'e owed you two or three.'

I meant to keep that ha'penny for the rest of my life. But one Friday night, after I'd walked part of the way to The Glue Pot with my Dad, I was so hungry I spent it on scrumps. I'm sure Uncle George would have approved. Well, I mean, that's what I'd always spent his ha'pennies on, wasn't it? I remember Mr Bulgarelli gave me a great shovel-full of scrumps. They lasted me all the way home. They were the best scrumps I ever had.

The Accumulator

Every Saturday morning I had to do it. From the time I was about nine until I was thirteen or fourteen, I should think. Every Saturday, regular as syrup of figs.

'Look at the clock,' our Mum would say.

'I can see it. I'm not blind.' Pulling up my grey, knitted socks and turning down the stripy bit at the top over the black elastic garters.

'I tell you what you will be if I gets any more o' your back-chat,' says our Mum, threatening me with the palm of her hand all covered in flour.

'All right, all right. Don't keep on at me. I'm goin', ain't I?'

'Ten minutes it'll take, no more. An' I want you straight back 'ere an' chop some sticks for me,' she would shout as I banged the back door behind me. I could still hear her chuntering on as I trotted off down the backs. 'An' don't you go takin' nothin' off 'er, remember. She's on the pension. Got nothin' to give away.'

As if I would. Well, I mean, I might have one of her rock cakes. That's not like accepting money, is it? I mean, she might be narked if I kept on refusing her rock cakes. As if I didn't like the look of 'em, or thought she couldn't cook or something.

[173]

My crikey! She could cook all right. I still reckon – all these years after – old Mrs Cook's rock cakes were the best I ever tasted. Cook by name and cook by nature, she was. My Mum baked a pretty good cake – specially jam sponges and what she called her mixed fruit special – but old Mrs C's rock cakes were something different. I never saw so many sultanas in one small rock cake. More fruit than cake it seemed to me. Which was as it should be, not like my Auntie Mary's fairy cakes, all pink crinkly paper cases and about two currants buried in half a ton of chaff.

But I never took money off old Mrs Cook, not once in all the years I did my Saturday morning good deed for the week.

'Go on, take a penny, lad,' she used to say, reaching in the folds of her voluminous black apron for her worn, leather purse.

'No, thank you, Mrs Cook,' I would say. 'I've 'ad me Friday penny from me Dad.'

'Then 'ave another one from me.'

'No, thank you. It wouldn't be right,' I'd say, my fingers clawing at the inside of my trousers pockets to stop from reaching out for the proffered penny.

'You're a good lad. I dunno what I'd do without you an' me wireless.'

It was the wireless that was the reason for my Saturday visit, actually. The big, oblong box made of dark brown, shiny wood with a big round dial like a clock face and three great knobs underneath, stood in the middle of the table on a kind of lace mat. It was the centre-piece of the room as indeed it was of the old lady's life. And it worked off an accumulator.

I hadn't the foggiest idea how the accumulator did it. All I knew was that nearly all the houses in our street were on electric but a few of the old people were afraid to have the new fangled invention in their homes and they stayed on the gas. For some reason it appeared you couldn't run a wireless set off the gas, so people like Mrs Cook had to have an accumulator to supply the juice. And the accumulator had to be changed every week. So that's where I came in.

Every Saturday the same old routine.

Knock! Knock!

'Who's there?'

''S only me, Mrs Cook.'

'Lift the latch an' come in then. Well, what a surprise. Fancy seein' you!'

'I come to change your accumulator, Mrs Cook.'

''Ave you reelly? Well, what a nice surprise.'

'Is it ready, Mrs Cook?'

'Just over there by the fireplace. An' the sixpence is on the corner o' the mantel-shelf.'

'Thank you, Mrs Cook.'

'You sure you can manage? It's a bit 'eavy. You quite sure?'

'It's all right, I c'n manage, ta. Don't get up. I'll shut the door be'ind me. Won't be gone more'n ten minutes.'

God, that accumulator wasn't half heavy! Nearly separated my arm from my body it did, lugging it round to Ellison's Electricals. It was a kind of big, square, glass bottle full of some greyish coloured stuff. It had a special handle to carry it by. It must have weighed a ton. Heavier even than one of my Aunt Mary's fairy cakes! The sort of electricity that you could buy in a thick glass jar really was heavy! I used to start off carrying it by the handle till my fingers went all numb and wouldn't grip any more. Then I carried it in my arms for a bit, hugging it to my chest like a mother with a precious glass baby. And all the way there and all

[175]

the way back I was scared stiff I'd drop it and smash it and it might explode and blow my legs off and then I'd be in a wheelchair and never play football again or go swimming out the gravel pits or . . . I clung on to the accumulator as if it was a bomb.

This particular Saturday, Snooky's gang were waiting for me just round the corner by the Co-op butchers.

'Whatcha got there, then, squirt?' asked Snooky, shoving me up against the wall. He was big and ugly with the first sprouting of a moustache and a perpetually runny nose.

I was petrified of Snooky. And his henchman, Fred Barker, a vicious, half-pint-sized, cross-eyed thug who did most of his fighting with his steel-tipped boots.

'You 'eard what Snooky said, dincha?' enquired Fred while I crouched against the wall and watched for his feet. 'What's tha' you got there?'

I waited till I saw the dreaded boot about to lash out, then I said, 'It's a bomb!'

Fred dropped his lethal foot and backed off a pace or two.

'Gerroff!' snarled Snooky, sniffing a glob of slime back up its nostril.

'All right, then, you jus' see.' I made as if to drop the accumulator.

Snooky edged back to the kerb where Fred and the rest of the gang hovered uncertainly.

'It ain't no bomb,' scoffed Fred.

'Well, what you standin' right back 'ere for, then?' countered Snooky. Sniff! Sniff! 'Why don't you go an' take it off of 'im?'

A period of silence. Snooky glowering at Fred. Fred avoiding the look. The rest of the gang shuffling and fidgeting behind them. Me, trapped against the wall, brain now working overtime trying to plot the next move. Fred, not sure if he's more afraid of Snooky's tongue or my bomb, took a tentative pace towards me. I summoned up the strength to lift my secret weapon head high as if to hurl it at him. And then the sixpence which I was holding pressed up against the side of the accumulator went and slipped through my fingers and rolled gently across the pavement right at Snooky's feet.

'Oo, look,' said Snooky, pointing. ''Is bomb's started coughin' up tanners!'

'Yeah, well,' muttered Fred. 'I'd rather 'ave a tanner than that ol' glass thing 'e's 'oldin', eh?'

He dropped a scruffy hand on the sixpence and Snooky pinned it to the ground with his right wellie.

''Oo said it was yourn, then, Fred Barker?'

'I was only gonna pick it up for you!'

''Oo's gang is this, then?'

'Yours, Snooky. It's yours. I reelly was gonna pick it up an' give it you. Honest I was!'

'OK then. You do that.'

Snooky lifted the sole of his wellie and Fred struggled with bruised fingers to pick up the coin.

'Gimme back me tanner,' I said bravely, though my voice wobbled a bit. 'It ain't mine. It – it – it belongs to an ol' lady.'

'Ho, ho, ho!' scoffed Snooky. 'Fancy that!'

'It belongs to an old lady,' mocked Fred. ''Ow d'you get 'old of it, then, if it belongs to an old lady? Eh? D'you rob 'er 'andbag?'

In an amalgam of fear and anger I found the strength to lift the accumulator above my head once more. Snooky, Fred and the rest of the gang were off down the street like six flashes of greased lightning.

'Gimme back me tanner,' I howled after them. 'I gotta 'ave it back. I gotta –'

I slithered down the Co-op wall and sat forlornly on

the pavement. I put down the accumulator by my side, partly because my arms were nearly worn out and partly to free the sleeve of my jersey to wipe my eyes. I wasn't crying – it was just that my eye liquid was overflowing!

I looked around. The street was deserted. Just me and the accumulator.

And no tanner! No sixpence to give the man at Ellison's Electricals in exchange for a freshly recharged accumulator. And no wireless for poor old Mrs Cook to listen to all next week.

Not if I could help it. I leaned back against the rough bricks and started to think. I was a fairly nifty thinker when needs be. What, I thought, would Humphrey Bogart or James Cagney or George Raft do in similar circumstances? Obviously, get another tanner from somewhere. How? Well – if not by fair means, it would have to be by foul. In this case, the end unquestionably justified the means. Who did I know who had sixpence which I could quickly and easily nick? Perhaps not nick – just borrow until I could raise enough by fair means to replace it. Who? Our Mum, of course. A boy's best friend. Where? In her purse in her handbag in the sideboard drawer. It would definitely only be borrowing. Definitely.

When I got to our back gate Mum was gassing to the woman that came round with the muffins every Saturday morning.

'Save me legs, will you?' said Mum when she set eyes on me. 'Slip indoors an' fetch me 'andbag out the sideboard, there's a good lad.'

I could hardly believe my luck.

'No point 'avin' a dog an' barkin' yerself, is it?' cackled the muffin woman as I hurtled up the path and into the house. I was back in two shakes of a lamb's tail.

[178]

'That was quick,' said Mum.

I gave her the bag, unable to look her in the eye, the sixpence scorching a hole in my trousers pocket. I picked up the accumulator from behind the coal bunk.

'What's that 'e 've got there?' asked Mrs Muffin.

'I dunno,' said Mum, fishing in her purse. 'I could've swore I 'ad a tanner in 'ere.'

I fled down the backway before she could accuse me. Not that she would have; it was just my guilty conscience. That was the worst of it, really. My Mum trusted me with her money, whatever else she might say about me, and I'd gone and let her down. Just temporarily. But I'd make it all right again when I put the sixpence back. There was no question about it being put back. There was only the question of when! But that could wait for a while. The immediate need was to get to Ellison's and back before old Mrs Cook threw a fit. If ever I was gone more than about a quarter of an hour, she was always sure I'd been run over by a Corporation double-decker. She used to carry on something alarming when I did get back about never forgiving herself, and what would me Mum do without me, and how much safer it was when they had the trams.

'Thought you was never comin',' said the man at Ellison's, taking the accumulator into the back room.

'Got 'eld up,' I muttered truthfully, fingering the row of coloured light bulbs on the counter.

''Ere we are, then.' He appeared with a fresh accumulator. 'An' cheap at the price, even if I say so as shouldn't.'

He shoved his fleshy palm at me. I dropped my Mother's sixpence into it. I felt much better, as if passing the stolen goods to someone else shifted the responsibility from my own unwilling shoulders.

'Where on earth you been?' scolded Mrs Cook. 'You

[179]

could've been knocked down by a Corporation bus an' what would your poor mother've done then, eh?'

'She'd prob'ly bin glad to see the back o' me,' I said absently, my mind still on the sixpence. It was really stupid the way this sixpence was bothering me. I mean, well, I'd knocked off a few odds and ends in my life – I wasn't any sort of angel – but I'd never before touched anything in my mother's handbag. That was sacred property. Like stealing from a church. She trusted me with her bag. 'Fetch me 'andbag for me, there's a good lad.'

'Mornin', Mr Allen,' I said to the grocer down the corner of Broad Street.

'Blimey!' said Mr Allen to his big, fat wife, just as if I wasn't there. 'D'you 'ear that? We are gettin' p'lite, ain't we? Last time I set eyes on 'im 'e was chuckin' me brussels sprouts all over the pavement.'

'Got any jobs, Mr Allen?' Still very polite.

'Jobs? You?' He went off into great guffaws of laughter. 'D'you 'ear the cheeky young devil? Any jobs! Can you imagine.'

I gave up being polite.

'I wouldn't work for you, anyway, Mister Tight-ass,' I yelled from the doorway. 'The only shop in the world where they cuts dolly mixtures in 'alf!'

I slammed the door so hard that the brass bell on its little spring rang out like a fire alarm. I snatched a handful of sprouts and kicked them in all directions up the street.

I tried the Co-op, the fish and chip shop, the coal yard, half-a-dozen corner shops, even the Chinese laundry. No one needed any odd jobs done. Not by me, at any rate.

I tried Mrs Edwards, Mrs Walker, my Auntie Nell and old Mrs Challis. No one wanted any errands run.

[180]

And by now I'd made this pledge with myself. I wasn't going home without that sixpence. Never mind how long it took. Even if I missed my dinner. And tea. Crikey, I thought, there might not be any tea, not if Mum hadn't had enough money left in her purse to pay Mrs Muffin.

I went and knocked on my best mate's front door.

'Is Albie comin' out to play?' I asked his Mum when she opened the door.

'I dunno,' she answered suspiciously. 'What sort o' trouble you plannin' today, eh? An' don't scrape them filthy shoes off on my clean step. Albie! Albie! Somebody 'ere wants you, Gawd knows why! An' don't you dare go out in them decent trousers. Not with 'im!'

'Albie,' I said, when we were perched comfortably on his back-yard wall. 'You got sixpence?'

He looked at me as if I'd asked for about a million pounds. 'Don't be daft,' he said eventually. 'I've 'ardly ever 'ad sixpence all at once in me life.'

'I gotta get sixpence somewhere,' I announced. And Albie gave me that special, knowing look that said he understood that this was something desperate and urgent and he would do his best to help me out.

'You tried all the usual?' he enquired.

I nodded.

'Shops?'

'Yeah, shops.'

'Neighbours?'

'Yeah, neighbours.'

'Your Auntie Nell?'

'I said ev'rybody, di'n't I?'

'Jars?'

'Eh?'

'Jars. You know – jam jars.'

I gave Albie one of my long-suffering, pitying

glances, the sort I reserved for people who were a bit touched in the head.

'What you on about! Jam jars!'

'Thinks you knows ev'rythin', don't you, Mr Clever Dick,' flamed Albie angrily. 'I s'pose you 'aven't 'eard they're payin' a penny a dozen for jam jars down the scrap-yard? You wants to stop clap-trappin' for a bit an' give your ears a chance, then you might 'ear somethin' for a change!'

'Jam jars!' I scoffed. 'What they want jam jars for?'

'I dunno,' said Albie. 'I don't care what they does with 'em, all I know is they pays a penny a dozen an' I'll bet you a million – no, ten million pounds I'm right.'

I remained silent. If Albie was prepared to stake ten million pounds on it he must know what he was on about.

After some minutes of rapid calculation I said, 'Blimey! That'll be seventy-two.'

'Eh?' said Albie, who was still in a smug sort of trance, having put one over on me.

'Seventy-two,' I repeated. 'Seventy-two jars we gotta find for me to get sixpence. I jus' worked it out.'

'You needn't swank, I could've worked it out if I wanted to. Anyway, it might as well be seventy-two thousand for all the chance we got of c'lectin' that many.'

'Oh! I dunno,' I said, sliding off the wall. 'I jus' thought o' summat. Come an' 'ave a look at these.'

Under the mangle and the old pram in the shed down our garden, laid out on the floor in neat rows, were all the jam jars in the world. At least, Albie thought so.

'Crikey! I never seen so many all together. Your Mam must 'ave been c'lectin' 'em ever since she went to school. You must 'ave jam for breakfast an' dinner an' tea an' supper ev'ry day to use all them jars!'

'I dunno what she's keepin' 'em for,' I said, surveying the rows of open glass mouths. 'She never chucks 'em away. Always washes 'em out an' sticks 'em out 'ere.'

Albie fetched his Dad's wheelbarrow. Not your conventional, one-wheeled, factory-made barrow but an incredible, four-wheeled, home-made contraption. A huge, square box knocked up out of timber pinched from various firms Albie's Dad had worked for. With an old pram wheel on each corner. And two bits of wood sticking out for handles.

Albie was very proud of his Dad's barrow even though it weighed half a ton and took two of us to push it with any degree of control. I couldn't help feeling my Dad had let me down badly, not being able to make a wheelbarrow like Albie's Dad. I don't think my Dad even realised how humiliating it was for me, being barrow-less and having to rely on Albie for transport.

We loaded the jars into the barrow taking care not to clunk them together. My mother was in the scullery ironing my Dad's Sunday shirt and she held the world record for hearing things she wasn't supposed to hear.

Shunting the barrow through our back gate was a bit tricky but eventually we were on our way down Cricklade Road heading for 'Junk' Jarvis's scrapyard.

'Gerroff the flamin' road, yer perishin' lunatics!' yelled a colourful assortment of bus drivers and delivery roundsmen (coal – bread – milk – fish – laundry – etc.).

We waved cheerily back to all of them, heads bent low over the handles as we trundled our barrowful of treasure under the railway bridges and over the cross-roads, happily ignoring the HALT sign and missing death under the wheels of a Typhoo Tea van by inches.

''Ow many?' enquired Junk, biting on the well-chewed stem of his briar pipe and smothering us in clouds of smoke.

[183]

'Seventy-two,' I said.

'Where d'you knock 'em off from?'

'They're not pinched,' I protested. 'They're ours. Our Mam bin savin' 'em up.'

'An' now she needs the money,' added Albie fiercely. 'Else she won't be able to afford no Sunday dinner!'

I thought that was going a bit far, saying things like that about our family. About his own family, maybe. But not ours.

'I'll give yer fourpence for 'em,' Junk said, peering into the barrow.

'A penny a dozen,' I objected.

'Tha's right,' Albie agreed.

'Fourpence,' said Junk.

'But that ain't fair,' I howled. 'Ev'rybody knows they're worth more 'n fourpence for all that lot. D'you think our Mam washed 'em an' got all the labels off jus' for a measly four blinkin' pence? Crikey! I 'spect the soap cost more 'n fourpence. An' the 'ot water. An' all the elbow grease what she used! I mean to say – well – an' then there's all the danger me an' 'im 'ave bin through gettin' 'em 'ere, riskin' our lives an' all that, as well as the pain I got in me side from the weight of that barrow. It feels like a ructure, as if me stomach's all worked loose. I s'pect I'll 'ave to 'ave an operation –!'

'All right! All right!' Junk gave in. 'If there's really seventy-two jars there, you can unload 'em in the shed over there an' ask young 'arold to count 'em an' I'll give you yer tanner on yer way out.'

We took turns at holding the tanner all the way home. First Albie pushed the truck and I rolled the smooth, shiny coin between finger and thumb; then I had a turn on the handles while Albie flicked the tanner spinning into the air and caught it expertly on the back of his hand.

'Don't go an' drop it down a drain,' I begged him.

'I never misses,' crowed Albie – and promptly missed.

He retrieved the precious sixpence from the gutter, polished it on one of several patches on the seat of his trousers, and handed it solemnly back to me.

'You better look after it,' he said. ''Cos when we passes Nash's sweet shop I'm gonna 'ave a job to stop meself goin' in an' buyin' one o' them new double-six choc'late bars what they've jus' brought out.'

We safely negotiated Nash's sweet emporium and I began to thank Albie for his loyal assistance. It tended to come out in stuttering phrases, unused as we were to anything resembling good manners.

'Ta for what you done, Albie. Well – I mean – thinkin' about the jars – an' lendin' us the barrow – an' 'elpin' push it – an' not goin' in Nash's – an' – 'n ev'rythin'. Nex' time I ever 'as any money that b'longs to me, I'll buy you a double-six, honest I will.'

I could hear our Mam and Dad yelling at each other as soon as I kicked open the back gate. They didn't go in for shouting matches as a rule. I wondered what this one was about.

'I'll wring 'is blasted neck when 'e does get 'ome,' thundered Dad.

'Not if I gets me 'ands on 'im first, you won't,' screeched Mam.

They were having a chat about me!

'Ever since last year I bin savin' them jars,' howled Dad. 'All ready for me piccalilli an' me pickled onions an' beetrots an' – an' –'

'An' 'oo washed 'em all up, eh?' added Mam. ''Oo scrubbed 'em an' got the labels off 'em an' put 'em all ready in the shed for when the bottlin' season come round, eh?'

'What's 'e want with the best part of an 'undred jars, anyway?' Dad exploded. 'If 'e's shootin' at 'em with that catapult of 'is 'e'll finish up with enough broken glass to fill the canal.'

'An' 'e've missed 'is dinner, too,' Mam went on. 'I'm not keepin' it warm for 'im no longer. It's goin' in the dustbin right now!'

I skipped out of the back gate the very tick I heard her hand on the latch. I went round the front and tapped on the window. When our kid heard me he came to the window and I signalled to him to let me in the front door.

'What's up?' he asked, opening the door an eighth of an inch.

'Sh! Jus' let me in an' shurrup.'

'Whaffor?'

'Never mind whaffor. It's my 'ouse as much as yourn. Gerrout the way!'

I shoved him aside and crept along the passage into the sitting-room. I could hear Mam and Dad out in the scullery still describing some of the tortures they were planning for me when they got their itching fingers round my throat! I opened the sideboard door and grabbed the handbag. With trembling fingers I snapped open the catch, took out the purse and popped in the tanner.

'Mam!' our kid cried out, pounding on the kitchen door with his hard little fists. 'Mam! Our big 'un's pinchin' money out o' your purse. Come quick, Mam!'

I didn't stop running until I reached the canal bridge. I spent the remaining hours of daylight contemplating suicide in two feet six inches of mud and slime. Albie came searching for me at dusk.

'Your Mam ain't 'alf carryin' on,' he informed me – as if I couldn't have guessed! 'Askin' ev'rybody up the street if they seen you anywhere. An' goin' on about workin' 'er fingers to the bone cookin' dinners for people as never comes 'ome, an' not 'avin' no pickled onions this year 'cos there ain't nothin' to put 'em in, an' bein' robbed by 'er own flesh an' blood –!'

Albie stopped suddenly, then gave me a quizzical sort of look and said, ''Ere, you ain't been robbin' your own flesh an' blood, 'ave you?'

I hurled half a brick into the murky water where it joined forces with several hundred others.

'Marvellous, ennit,' I expostulated. 'The firs' time in me life I try to be like Robin 'ood – or St George – or somebody like that, they goes an' says I'm robbin' 'em! I was puttin' it *in*, not takin' it *out* – an' don't look at me like that or I'll punch your 'ead! I tell you I was bein' honest! More honest than I ever been in me life. But not any more, I'm not. From now on I'm gonna be more like James Cagney an' Humphrey Bogart an' the Dead End Kids. I'll finish up in San Quentin an' they'll be sorry 'bout accusin' me of what I ain't done. An' they'll ask for a free pardon an' they'll be too late 'cos I'll 'ave already gone to the 'lectric chair!'

I ran out of words. Albie fished in his pocket and brought out a couple of furry lemon drops.

'Ain't you 'ad nothin' to eat all day? 'Ere you are.'

I took one of the lemon drops, picked off some of the fur and sucked it lovingly between my teeth.

''Ave 'em both,' said Albie. 'We 'ad new bread an' lemon curd for tea.'

My stomach groaned at the mention of food.

'I'm prob'ly never goin' 'ome again,' I confided to Albie.

'I s'pect you will,' he said.

I expect I must have done.

[187]

Arsenal v Sheffield Wednesday

The crocodile must have been a quarter of a mile long. By the time the stragglers shuffled through the school gates the vanguard – me and Vic – were down by the bus stop outside the Fifty Shilling Tailors.

'Didn't I tell you not to go racing on like that?' screamed Mr Hardy, the games master, generally referred to as Oliver, of course.

'We ain't racin',' I said meekly, while Vic pretended to be weighing up the fifty-shilling suits in the window. 'Only I thought as 'ow we'd never get nowhere the speed some of 'em goes.'

'Button your lip!' Oliver said. 'And wait here till the rest of 'em catch up.'

He belted off up the road, yelling and waving his arms like a madman.

'Come on, you lot. There won't be any time left for a games lesson at this rate. I've met snails that could give you lot fifty yards start in a hundred and thrash the tails off you!'

Every Thursday, Standard V had football down the recreation ground behind the carriage and wagon works. Apart from Saturday – which you couldn't really count as an ordinary day of the week – I lived from Thursday to Thursday that winter of thirty-eight. I was twelve and I was in Standard V and that meant I was old enough to have football. Every Thursday. Unless it rained. Please God, let it be the driest winter on record.

'Right. Now lead on properly this time,' Oliver said. 'I'm bringing up the rear. And if you go off like a pair of greyhounds again, I'll cuff your ears when I get you down that rec!'

Vic and I moved off again at a steady, military sort of pace. We wore our football jerseys round our necks, tied by the sleeves, and our boots slung from our shoulders by the knotted laces. We were the fortunate ones, having jerseys and boots. Mind you, we'd worked for 'em. It took me three months of running errands for a ha'peny a time to save up enough to buy Harold Briggs's boots, second-hand, for one and a tanner. And I dug old Mrs Cook's bit of back garden twice before she gave me her eldest son's old jersey. He played for the Holy Cross Street Workingmen's Club – same shirts as Arsenal, red with white sleeves. It came down to my ankles. I looked like a pillar box with arms! I managed to tuck several feet of it into the baggy, off-white shorts which my Mum had made for me out of an old sheet.

'Stop dawdling at the front!' bellowed Oliver from the tail of the crodocile.

'Blimey!' muttered Vic. ''E wants to make 'is blasted mind up, don't 'e?'

As soon as we had crossed the road at the halt sign on the corner by the shirt factory, and left the main street and the crowds of shoppers and the buses and vans behind us, we broke into a trot. Even Oliver couldn't have held us back once we got the scent of the turf in our nostrils. In fact, he would end up racing us down

[189]

the footpath that led to the rec. He loved his football as much as we did – and I reckon he looked forward to getting out of that dingy, depressing school as much as we did, too. He was the only young one on a staff of grumpy, grizzled old men.

'Get changed quick, then,' he shouted. 'First two ready can pick sides.'

The hedge was our dressing-room. It offered scant shelter from the icy, north-east wind which swept straight from the Russian steppes across our rec. We pressed up close under the bare, spiky branches and put on whatever kit we had. A few had proper football boots; most had an old pair of ordinary, black boots that were too far gone for everyday use; those who had nothing suitable to change into had been left behind to do extra arithmetic with Mr Partridge.

We sported a motley collection of jerseys, most of them passed down from older brothers or men who lived up the street and played for one of the local clubs. They were faded and torn under the arms and flopped open at the neck where there should have been a lace to tie up.

'Well done, Victor, lad,' said Oliver, as Vic sprinted out of the hedge. 'You'll be one captain. Go and get some coats down.'

Vic returned to the hedge and scooped up an armful of clothes. Then he raced off towards the gas works railings and made two piles exactly eight giant strides apart. He returned for further supplies of surplus garments and scooted off to make the other goal a hundred yards away towards the factory wall.

'How much longer you lot going to be?' shrieked Oliver, hopping from one foot to the other, his face all pink and blue with the cold. 'You're like a lot of old ladies getting ready for a fancy dress ball.'

I waited until Fred Gisby was ready before I made my appearance. He could be the other captain. Then Vic would have first pick because he'd been first one ready; he would pick me; and between us we'd show 'em the way round. I wasn't daft! And I never liked being on the losing side even in friendlies.

Choosing sides was a long-drawn-out ritual, mostly because neither captain wanted the last half-dozen kids left who were useless and only got in the way or cried if they got kicked on the shins. Eventually we lined up, twenty-four-a-side!

'We're Sheffield Wednesday,' announced Fred Gisby who sported a blue-and-white striped shirt that looked old enough to have been worn by the centre-forward of Noah's Ark United.

'We don't mind,' said Vic, generously. 'We're Arsenal, anyway.' There was a preponderance of red jerseys in our team.

'Where we playing?' asked Oliver, all sarcastic. 'Highbury or Hillsborough?'

He blew a shattering blast on the whistle which he wore on a bit of string round his neck. Vic side-footed the ball to me and we were off on my weekly excursion through the Elysian Fields.

'Pass it! Pass it!'

'Out to the wing! Give it to Snowy!'

'Let Nobby 'ave it!'

'Throw in,' yelled Oliver.

'It ain't gone out yet!' said Vic.

'You'll be gone out in a minute!' Oliver rushed up to Vic, wagging his finger very professional like. 'Button up or you've had your last games lesson till after Christmas. Try playing with your feet instead of your mouth!'

Oliver picked up a loose ball in midfield and began to dribble through our massed defence.

'That ain't fair, sir,' complained Arsenal.

'I'll play a bit for both sides,' Oliver reassured us.

He wasn't a bad player and being twice as big as most of us he could barge us out of his way even when he couldn't dribble round us. He scythed through us – but he was basically a very understanding sort of teacher because he rarely showed off by scoring himself. He generally passed to somebody else when he got in front of goal.

'Here, Fred. You can't miss this one.'

He slipped a perfect, rolling pass into Fred Gisby's stride and Fred, who could play a bit himself, hammered the ball just inside the left-hand pile of coats.

'Goal!' roared the twenty-four Sheffield Wednesday players.

'Foul! Offside! Free-kick!' protested Arsenal.

'Goal,' proclaimed Oliver, pointing back to the centre.

'But it 'it the post,' Vic cried. 'I seen it. It flipped the sleeve o' Spud's jacket.'

'I've warned you once this afternoon about disputing the referee's decision,' hissed Oliver.

Vic looked to me to carry on the battle for him.

'It did, sir,' I chipped in. 'I seen it. It jus' scraped against the jacket.'

'And what is my rule?' Oliver bent forward. I could feel his warm breath on my face and I knew I should feel his hand warming my back-side if I didn't watch out.

'Please, sir, I thought the rule was –' I chose my words carefully – 'if it touches the coats, it ain't a goal.'

I backed away a pace or two in case he took a swipe at me.

But he only ground his teeth and ranted. 'You never listen to anything I say, do you? None of you! I always said, if it touches the inside of the coats, it's a goal. Like

[192]

it had gone in off the post. Right? Understand? All you thickies got it clear?'

We trooped back to the middle of the pitch to restart the game.

''E can't see the diff'rence between the ball actually 'ittin' the coats or jus' touchin' 'em,' Vic whispered in my ear. 'I wonder they lets 'im out without a white stick an' a guide dog!'

'What d'you say?' snapped Oliver.

'Nothin', sir,' said Vic, with eyes as soft and innocent as a baby calf.

'Get off!' Oliver pointed to the hedge as if he was performing at Wembley.

'But –'

'No buts! Get off. An' if you open your mouth again I'm reporting you to Mr Lockwood in the morning and it'll be three on each hand for you, in Prayers, in front of the whole school.'

Vic shambled off, two-thirds of his beloved games period cruelly snatched from him.

'We ain't got no chance, now,' I groaned. 'One nil down an' Vic gone off.'

'He should have thought of that before he started clap-trapping,' said Oliver. 'Anyway, I'm on your side now.'

We pressed on with the match, leaving Vic to freeze in silence under the hedge. It was so cold nobody wanted to stand about in their proper positions so we chased after the ball like bees round a jam pot. Sometimes there must have been about forty of us within spitting distance of the muddy pudding which was getting so heavy none of us could shift it more than five or six yards.

Oliver suddenly emerged from the swarm with the ball at his feet.

[193]

'Come on, then,' he bawled, charging off downfield. 'Get it off me if you can! Tackle me! Come on! What are you scared of? Hey! Watch it! Don't tackle from behind like that! Don't tackle –!'

The rest of the sentence was lost in the mud as Oliver pitched headlong into the quagmire. He slid along on his face and stomach, legs splayed, arms outstretched, like some giant bird making a forced landing. We stood like statues – all except Des Hacker, who had dared to trip Sir in full flight. Des was already a speck on the horizon!

'Who did it?' Oliver sat in the squelching morass and scraped mud out of his eyes and mouth. 'Who? Just own up whoever it was.'

As though anyone was likely to do that! On the other hand, nobody was going to split on Des either. Not with Oliver in the sort of temper he was in.

'Who?' he repeated softly. I knew from bitter experience that soft was much worse than loud in certain circumstances. 'If I do not find who tripped me up within ten seconds we are going back to school and do tables till five o'clock and you've seen the last of this rec. for the year!'

No one spoke. Unless he noticed Des was missing there seemed no way out. I could hear the seconds ticking away deafeningly in my head. Tables till five! No more games lessons! The end of the world closing in fast!

'Please, Mr Hardy, it was me. I sort of ran across your legs from the back and it sort of made you fall down. But I didn't mean to, sir! It was an accident.'

We all stared aghast at Sidney Sealey. Little Sidney Sealey. The midget of our class. All fair, curly hair and rolled-down socks. Played the violin and hated football. Only came to games lessons because his mother said he needed the fresh air.

'I don't believe you, Sidney.' Oliver got slowly to his

feet and clawed the gooey mud off the knees of his trousers.

We all waited trembling on Sidney's reply. Would he go through with it and persist in his lie in order to save the class from instant punishment or would he back down?

'But you said somebody had to own up in ten seconds or else,' Sidney said without batting an eyelid. 'So I did.'

Oliver considered for a while. He didn't believe for one second that little Sidney had brought him down – and he knew that we knew it, too. But he was also impressed with Sidney's brave effort to save the rest of us from retribution.

'Well, now,' he said, 'if it was an accident – and I sincerely hope it was – accidents do happen, and there's nothing in the Football Association rules to cover accidents, so you'd best stop gawking and get on with the game.'

Oh, he could be very understanding, could Oliver! Very. And he went up in our estimation a thousand per cent. Just to prove what a jolly good bloke he was, he called Vic out of his premature retirement under the hedge and reinstated him as captain of Arsenal.

'And don't forget, it's your very last chance.' He wagged a warning finger under Vic's nose.

'I won't forget,' Vic promised happily. 'Honest! I won't say nothin' to nobody all the rest o' the match.'

Oliver awarded himself a free-kick and we allowed him to take it without protest. He scored with a tremendous shot and we all clapped and cheered and cried, 'Blimey! What a goal!' and such-like things. Oliver managed a mud-stained grin and we trotted back to the centre of the field to restart the game.

Sidney Sealey, having collected more matey slaps on

the back and promises of eternal friendship than he had known in his life previously, immediately lost all interest in the football and returned to his position near the hedge (outside left) from whence he could watch the tank engines shunting wagons in the gas works yard.

And Des Hacker, the arch criminal, unaware of Sidney's brave intervention on his behalf, hid cowering in Spackman's coal-yard, half a mile away, afraid to go home and even more afraid to come back.

'Half-time!' shrieked Oliver, giving a very professional blast on his whistle and a dramatic gesture towards the hedge. We rushed for the meagre protection from the freezing wind that the hedge offered and huddled into it, all mud and sweat and steaming breath, while Oliver lectured us on the finer points of the game.

'Rubbish!' he cried. 'Never seen such a lot of cissies in my life! All wrapped up together you wouldn't make half a footballer! Now get out there and let's have a bit of action! And keep to your positions! And no more mouth! Right?'

'Right,' said Vic, leading the sides back on to the stadium. I trotted out behind him, trying to imitate the hunch-shouldered, rolling gait of the pros I watched on Saturday afternoons. Sheffield Wednesday, in the person of Fred Gisby, kicked off, and Part Two of the Thursday Spectacular got under way.

As the afternoon wore on the pace of the game slowed considerably. Weighed down with pounds of clinging mud – muscles aching – hearts thumping – lungs bursting – we slogged away, unwilling to give in but hardly able to go on. Only Oliver, with his longer legs and greater stamina, was still ploughing through the churned-up muck like a young racehorse.

'Come on,' he yelled. 'What's up with you? Got about as much go in you as a crate-load of three-legged, rheumatic tortoises! And come back, Fred Gisby, you're three miles off-side!'

Fred Gisby came back, reluctantly, and Oliver placed the ball for the free-kick. Then he stood with one foot on it while he waved us into position.

'Ten yards off! And spread out a bit. You look like a mother's meeting all stood together like that! Open out!'

He took his foot off the ball and did a very swanky back-heel, calling out to the goalkeeper as he did so, 'Your ball, goalie.'

The only trouble was – there was no goalkeeper there. Only two piles of coats and a great space between them.

'Goal!' crowed Fred Gisby. ''E've gone an' scored in 'is own goal!'

Oliver's face was a study.

'Where is he?' he spluttered. 'Where's that idiot Jackson gone?'

'I 'spect 'e've gone for a widdle,' Vic suggested.

'A what?' Oliver exploded.

''E means a wee,' I nipped in quickly. I'd had a more refined upbringing than Vic! 'You know, sir – a hedge ticket!'

Jacko duly appeared from behind the hedge, hoisting up his shorts. When he saw the throng gathered around his goal and realised his absence had not gone unnoticed, he came scampering back as fast as his podgy little legs would carry him. He was built a bit like a football, was Jacko – a perfectly round body ruined by arms and legs sticking out all over the place, and surmounted by a flat, fried-egg of a face.

'Where the dickens d'you think you've been?' Oliver asked in his deadly, quiet voice.

'I – um – I – well – I 'ad to go!' Jacko said, quite simply and honestly.

'Oh! you did, did you? Did you hear that, everybody?

Jackson had a sudden call!' Oliver waxed sarcastic. 'Does anyone remember the last time Frank Swift had to leave his goal at Wembley for a few minutes to answer the call of nature?'

'Nobody called,' said Jacko. 'I just 'ad to go for a number one!'

'Any more cheek out o' you, Jackson, and you'll disappear for ever!' Oliver poked Jacko in his fat stomach. 'I'll burst your bubble!'

We all fell about laughing.

'Right! We'll have a change of goalie, then. We'll have somebody reliable. Come on, Bristow –' he beckoned Roy Bristow to him – 'you can take over in goal. And you, Jackson, get up in the forward line. You'll do less harm there.'

'But, sir,' protested Roy, 'I can't play in goal! I'm a natural, ball-playing, tricky, Alex James-type inside forward!'

Oliver took two paces towards Roy, who promptly obliged by going in goal.

'Right! Now I'm going to re-take the free kick,' announced Oliver.

'But, sir,' Vic blurted out, forgetting he was on borrowed time.

I rushed to his rescue. 'Sir!' I pleaded. 'You've already took it an' scored an own goal. You can't take it again. It's not fair!'

'Not fair!' Oliver screeched, tweaking my frozen left ear between his finger and thumb. 'What d'you mean, not fair? D'you know more about the rules than me? Eh? Didn't you know, Mister Clever Dick, you can't score an own goal direct from a free kick?'

I didn't argue because I wanted to keep my left ear intact but I felt sure he was wrong. I still reckon he was. One day I'm gong to look it up in the F.A. rules.

Anyway, he took the free kick again and the epic contest continued.

We played on until the light started to fade. Oliver blew a ferocious blast on his whistle and pointed to the hedge. There was a chorus of protest.

'Sir, we can't stop now. It's six each. Can't we play extra time? Jus' till somebody gets the winner? Please, sir!'

'What we gonna play by?' grinned Oliver. 'Moonlight?'

Oliver was always in a good mood after the game. While we sat under the hedge and changed, he talked to us non-stop. About how we'd played. About the England team. About the goal he saw Tommy Lawton score. Anything as long as it was football. And if our frozen fingers were too numb to untie our laces, he'd undo them for us, kneeling in front of us as we offered up our muddy boots to him.

'Come on, then,' he would say suddenly. 'I've got a home to go to even if you lot haven't. Anybody going back by the main road can walk with me if you like. The rest of you get on home a bit sharp and don't get into any trouble on the way.'

A few of us always walked back the main road way, even though it was the long way round, just to be with Oliver. There weren't many teachers I'd have been seen dead with. Oliver was the only one I would positively choose to walk with, especially when he was in this warm, chatty mood on a Thursday afternoon.

'You ever seen Stanley Matthews in real life?' Vic asked him.

'Is it true, sir, 'Arry 'Ibbs is the smallest goalie there ever was?' somebody else was enquiring.

'Sir,' I said, because I was one of those annoying kids who wouldn't leave things well alone, 'about that free-kick that you put through your own goal –'

'One at a time,' Oliver pleaded, not hearing what any of us said because we were all yapping away together. 'I can't listen to ten of you all at once.'

We were passing Spackman's coal-yard.

'I went to Hampden Park once,' Oliver was saying to his goggle-eyed fan club. 'England versus Scotland. On the overnight sleeper from King's Cross.'

I couldn't have been more impressed if he'd said he walked to the North Pole.

'Left London at ten o'clock Friday night and was eating breakfast in a caff in Glasgow before eight. Best porridge I ever tasted. Not like that muck your mothers shove into you lot, out of a packet. Real porridge. And kippers.'

'Kippers!' we echoed. 'Ugh! Porridge an' kippers.'

'You lot dunno what's good for you. You ought to –' Oliver broke off abruptly, whipped into Spackman's yard, dashed round behind a mountain of freshly-dumped coal, and came out the other side clutching a small dishevelled body wrapped in an outsize black-and-white striped jersey.

'Well, well! Fancy finding this behind a coal tip,' said Oliver. 'A fugitive from Newcastle United! You lost your first team place or something?'

Des Hacker just stood there, shivering from head to foot with fear and cold.

'Lost your voice, have you, Hacker? Nothing to say?'

'No, sir,' mumbled Des.

'You usually spend your evenings in coal-yards disguised in football togs, eh?'

'No, sir.'

'How long were you planning on staying there?'

'Dunno, sir,'

'I think you're a bit thick, Hacker. Hiding there all night wouldn't do you much good, would it? You'd have to come to school tomorrow morning and face the music.'

'What sort of music?' asked Vic, dim as ever.

'You know what I mean, don't you, Hacker?' Oliver purred, bending significantly to rub the still muddy patches on the knees of his trousers.

You could have heard us gasp a mile away. All eyes on Des. He was shivering fit to fall apart.

'You're a terrible late tackler, Hacker. You'd do well in the Third Division North, you would. Clogger Hacker.'

We watched Oliver's face closely, not able to judge from the tone of voice the degree of anger he was feeling.

'No good running away from life, is it, Hacker? Got to stop and take what's coming sometime. Right?'

'Yes, sir,' mumbled Des, lip trembling, eyes brimming.

'Can't walk home like that, Hacker, can you? Not in that mucky football rig-out. Where's your clothes?'

'Back there,' Des pointed towards the rec. 'Under the hedge.'

'Better go and get dressed, then, hadn't you? If someone hasn't pinched your stuff.'

Des gave a great sob and stumbled away down the road.

'Hacker!' yelled Oliver. 'Come here!'

Des wavered.

'Do as you're told.'

Des turned.

'You'll freeze to death wandering around like that. Come here and put on something respectable.'

Oliver reached under his jacket and pulled out a bundle of clothes. Des's jumper and trousers, shirt and boots. He tossed them into Des's arms.

[201]

'Better nip round behind the coal again and dress yourself, Hacker, eh? Can't do it out here in the main road, can we?'

Suddenly, Oliver laughed. A lovely, lovely sound. We all joined in, pleased for Des and proud of Oliver.

I tell you, there weren't many teachers like Mr Hardy in those days. Not many at all.

Me and Humphrey Bogart

'Where we goin' this afternoon?' asked Albie, sitting on our coal-bunk, pulling up his grey socks which his Mum knitted, always about three sizes too big.

'What d'you mean, where we going?' said Vic.

'You know what I mean. Which one?'

There were six choices. The Arcadia, the Empire, the Palace, the Palladium, the Regent or the Rink.

'The Palace,' announced Spud, bunking himself up to sit astride our back-gate. 'We'll go to the Palace. It's Charlie Chan.'

'If you don't get off that gate our Dad'll thump you, Spud,' I said. 'It won't shut proper with you keep climbin' on it.'

'We've seen it,' said Georgie.

'No we 'aven't, neither.'

'Yes we 'ave,' said Vic with authority. 'All the Charlie Chans what comes to the Palace are second time round. We've seen 'em all.'

'It's Sonja Henie at the Arcadia,' suggested Albie, tentatively.

'Well!' exploded Spud, nearly falling off the back-gate. 'I never 'spected to 'ear you suggest we went to see 'er. Well, I mean – fancy you wantin' to see 'er again.

[203]

We seen 'er about fifteen times an' she jus' does the same ev'ry time. Jus' skates round an' round an' round an' nothin' never 'appens.'

'Well, I like 'er,' Albie said.

'You can 'ave 'er for all I care.'

'I can't go to the Arcadia, anyway,' said Vic. 'I got sent 'ome by the school nurse las' time we went to the Arcadia. Our Ma said I picked 'em up there. Alive, I was. Crawlin' all over –'

'All right, all right,' I interrupted. 'We don't wanna go into all that again.'

I was always very squeamish about vermin. My mother would never have let me go out with Vic again if she knew he was susceptible to fleas.

'There's a George Formby at the Rink,' Georgie offered, almost apologetic. He was two years younger than the rest of us – only in our gang because he was left-footed and owned a three-spring cricket bat – and not permitted to take part in any serious decision-making.

'You gotta be in a kind o' special mood for George Formby,' said Spud. 'An' I ain't in it!'

Vic took the lid off the dustbin and rooted out a copy of the local evening paper.

'It's Bette Davis at the Palladium,' he announced eventually.

'Well, I ain't gonna see 'er never again.' It was my turn to blow off. 'She ain't nice-lookin' an' she ain't funny an' it seems to me it's the same film every time you sees 'er.'

'She can't skate, neither,' said Albie.

'I'd rather –' I tried to think of the deadliest thing you could do on a Saturday afternoon – 'I'd rather go up town with our Mum than see Bette Davis!'

'I was only readin' out loud,' complained Vic. 'I can't

go to the Palladium anyway. The bloke in the peaked cap still remembers me. Well, I mean, I di'n't know that fat, ol' usherette 'ad a tray full of ice-cream when I run into 'er –'

'That leaves the Regent an' the Empire,' said Spud.

'It's some soppy kids' film at the Empire,' Georgie informed us. 'It can't be no good 'cos our Mum said I ought to go an' see it!'

I could hardly believe my luck! It would have to be the Bogart film and I had not needed to use any of my considerable powers of persuasion!

'We'll 'ave to go to the Regent,' wailed Spud. 'I 'ates the Regent. I 'ates the Mighty Wurler!'

'Wurlitzer,' Georgie corrected him, somewhat diffidently. 'The Mighty Wurlitzer.'

'I 'ates it whatever it's called. I 'ates organs.'

'Prob'ly 'cos 'e's such a rotten organiser!' I said. Nobody laughed. The debate was too serious.

'Never mind, Spud,' Albie comforted him. 'At least it's a big place. We can sit a long way back. An' we're sure to get in easy.'

Vic folded the paper and replaced it in the dustbin. 'It's all right for some,' he said.

He knew I was nuts about Humphrey Bogart.

'It's a gangster picture, ennit?' enquired Georgie.

'Sure. A good 'un.' I knew I had Georgie on my side. 'They reckon there's about twenty gets shot when Cagney and Bogart breaks out o' San Quentin.' That should stir up the bloodthirsty side of Spud's nature. 'An' I think the other picture on with it is Deanna Durbin.' That should please Albie if he couldn't have Sonja Henie. And I could probably find something else to do while she was on!

'What time's it start?' asked Spud.

'You're a crafty 'un, you are. Got your own way

[205]

without sayin' a word,' said Vic, who liked having his way almost as much as me. 'My Mum always said you'll go far. Dartmoor, I shouldn't be surprised!'

We met by the lamp-post outside Albie's house at half-past one, and it was teeming with rain. The Regent opened its dors at one forty-five prompt and the supporting film came on at two.

We went to the pictures every other Saturday afternoon in summer (in winter football took preference) from about 1936 until the war came and separated us irrevocably. Every fortnight, May to September, regular as a dose of chocolate laxative. Actually, there was a kids' matinee Saturday mornings – 'the twopenny rush' – but we wouldn't have been found dead there. All good, virtuous, moral stuff – Mickey Mouse, The Three Stooges, Roy Rogers, Robin Hood, Gene Autry . . .

Not for us! Not on your nellie! Who wants to go to the pictures with a thousand squealing kids?

When we arrived at the Regent, Frankenstein, the commissionaire with the big boots and square head, was just opening the glass doors and ushering in the straggly queue. We huddled out of the deluge in the porch of the Baptist Church to count our communal wealth.

'Tenpence,' I announced.

'That all?' Vic peered at the copper collection in the palm of my hand.

'I won't come, then,' said Spud, nobly – but knowing full well we'd never let anyone stand down for the sake of a few coppers. 'I couldn't get no money this week now our Dad's on the dole.'

'It's all right,' I said. 'It'll mean two in the front an' three round the back. An' that'll leave tuppence for sweets.'

'OK,' said Vic. 'You an' me in front 'cos we're biggest.'

'An' got the most cheek,' added Albie.

'Experience,' Vic said.

So Vic and I took up strategic positions on the pavement outside the plate glass doors while the other three strolled off round the block to the rear of the cinema.

'Don't be too long,' yelled Albie. 'We'll get soaked waitin' down that alley-way.'

'Depends on other people, don't it,' muttered Vic, sizing up the adults who were converging on the entrance.

You see, Humphrey Bogart films were 'A' certificate. All the films worth seeing were 'A', come to think of it. Some right babyish junk got 'U' rating in those days. So we could only get in if we were accompanied by an adult.

'Take us in, mister.' Vic put on his most respectful voice. 'Please mister. I got me fourpence.'

He was a young chap, on his own, wearing his first trilby hat and Burton's pin-stripe suit and black patent shoes. He took Vic's fourpence without pausing in his stride. He knew the form. He'd been one of us not too long back. Without a word he and Vic moved into the foyer. The young man bought the tickets, gave them to the usherette at the foot of the stairs – and his short, silent acquaintance with Vic was over, as they made their separate ways into the auditorium.

The law had been complied with! Vic had been accompanied into the cinema by a person over eighteen years of age. Everyone knew it was a fiddle. Frankenstein knew, standing there in his admiral's uniform, watching it all going on right under his nose. The manager knew, hovering like a head-waiter in his dress suit, seeing everything, saying nothing. The cashier knew, the usherettes knew – all the world knew. How many tens of thousands of kids up and down the country were asking complete strangers to take them into the cinema without realising the risk they were taking in order to get round a stupid law? I certainly never realised it then. I just couldn't understand why the manager didn't simply come outside, collect all the fourpences and take us in himself. The law would presumably have been satisfied – and the pavement would have looked a lot tidier!

'Take us in please, mister.' It was an unwritten law of our own (not the country's) that we inflicted ourselves on our benefactors singly. So there was Vic inside and me outside and not getting any luck either.

'Please, Mrs –' I was getting desperate when I started asking ladies – 'will you take me in with you? I've got the money.'

After what seemed like hours and was probably about ten minutes, I made it. The usherette led me right down the front where I spotted Vic in a seat in the second row with his legs occupying a seat in the front row.

'If 'e's with you,' the usherette hissed in my ear, 'tell 'im to get 'is mucky feet down or I'll get Frankenstein to come in an' throttle 'im!'

The lights went down the moment I got settled in and the second feature film began. But Vic and I had more important business afoot than watching rubbish like Deanna Durbin.

Vic went first – softly, unobtrusively. I lost sight of him in the darkness. Then I saw a thin shaft of light as he pushed aside the heavy curtain under the dimly-lit, red sign – GENTS AND EXIT. I gave him two minutes and then followed. We met in the toilet. No words exchanged – we knew the drill well enough. Vic posted himself close to the curtain where he could intercept any-one heading for the gents, while I nipped smartly down the corridor to the double green exit doors. They were the sort that had a heavy iron bar across the inside which you pushed up to let yourself out. They couldn't be opened from the outside.

I heaved up the bar, Albie heard me and gave a shove. The door opened a few inches, Albie slid through and into the toilet. A short pause – no warning signal from Vic – and up went the bar again and little Georgie came wrig-gling through. Only one more to go – my heart was thudding like Tommy Lawton was inside my chest prac-tising penalties with it! I had a conscience. I knew I was doing wrong. But the excitement made up for the shame.

I slammed up the bar once more. Spud's black shoe, with the toe-cap gaping like the entrance to Box Tunnel, eased through the gap. Then I heard Vic.

'Oh! Excuse me, mister. I've dropped a sixpence some-where. It's a bit dark out 'ere. You got a match?'

I kicked Spud's ankle, closed the doors as quietly as possible and hared back into the toilet.

'Can't see it nowhere,' we heard Vic going on. 'P'raps I dropped it in the lav.'

'Better go an' 'ave a look, then,' came a man's voice. When he and Vic came into the toilet, there was Albie and Georgie, both wet through, and me standing in a line as innocent looking as new-born babes and not a piddle between us!

'Fancy anybody wantin' to go to the lav as soon as that,' said Vic when the man had gone. 'The picture's 'ardly started.'

'P'r'aps they ain't got one at 'ome,' sniggered Albie.

'Else 'e've been down the pub,' suggested Georgie. 'If my Dad goes down the pub Sat'day dinner-time, 'e's up an' down the garden all afternoon.'

'Don't forget Spud,' I reminded them. ''E'll be half drowned out there.'

'Is it Deanna Durbin, the little picture?' enquired Georgie. Vic and I nodded glumly. ''E'll be better off half drowned out there in that case!' said Georgie.

Vic returned to his post.

I went back to the exit.

I lifted the bar gingerly. Spud charged. I fell back. The double doors crashed open against the stone walls.

'What the 'eck!' I spluttered.

'I'm near drowned,' howled Spud, as wet as if he'd just come out of the boating lake up the park.

'Shurrup, you stupid twits.' Vic came along the passage.

'Nobody could've 'eard,' said Spud. Then, seeing Albie and Georgie peering round the corner, he added: 'Could they?'

'Into the lav, quick,' I said, shoving the doors back in place.

We waited anxiously. No sign of Frankenstein! Deanna Durbin must have been going full blast!

'Let's go inside!' Spud pleaded.

'Don't rush it,' I soothed him. 'You'll spoil it all if you don't take your time.'

'Let 'im go first,' said Georgie kindly.

So Spud was the first to make his way nonchalantly into the cinema. We followed at one minute intervals. We all met up in the centre of Row M which was the shilling seats about half-way back. Well, I mean to say, who could stick the second row from the front all afternoon? Looking up at the screen nearly broke your neck and Fred Gutteridge on the Mighty Wurlitzer nearly perforated your ear-drums!

We chatted our way through the Deanna Durbin film – except Albie, who was going through this difficult period and kept getting crushes on Judy Garland and Eleanor Powell and Snow White and Sonja Henie . . . and for the next few days, Deanna Durbin, judging by the mushy look on his face.

'Is it 'umphrey Bogart now?' asked Georgie as Miss Durbin faded into the sunset and the gauze curtains swished across the screen.

'Not yet,' I told him. 'We ain't 'ad the News yet.'

The news – British Movietone complete with Leslie Mitchell – was dead crummy apart from the car racing at Brooklands and a few murky shots of Wally Hammond smashing the Aussies all over Trent Bridge in the Test Match.

'Now?' asked Georgie.

'Nearly,' I replied. 'Just the trailers.'

'What's trailers?'

'Bits o' what's on nex' week.'

After the bits of next week's film the lights went up.

'I thought you said –' Georgie began.

'It's the interval, ennit? You gotta 'ave a interval. So as Fred can get in 'is practice on the Wurlitzer!'

'And so as they can get rid o' their sweets an' ice-creams. 'Ere, Vic, we still got tuppence left.'

'I know. What'll I get, then?'

'Sharp's toffees.'

'Fruit gums.'

'Trebor mints.'

'I'll see what she've got,' said Vic and went off to inspect the usherette's tray of sweets. By the time he returned the lights were beginning to dim.

'Now?' asked Georgie.

'Now!' I said.

'Right, you lot. Out of it!' hissed a man's voice in the gangway.

'What ?'

[211]

'You 'eard! C'mon, all on you – up the office!'

'But we ain't –'

'You tell the manager all about it, eh? C'mon, I don't want no trouble.'

We edged out of our seats and followed, meekly, as Frankenstein led us into the foyer, through the baize door marked STAFF ONLY, and into the holy of holies, the manager's office.

The head waiter sat behind a huge mahogany desk, like a presiding magistrate in a Hollywood film, but even more alarming for us was the sight of a police sergeant, helmet in crook of arm, standing at the corner of the desk like the first witness for the prosecution.

'Well?' the manager asked, raising his eyebrows in a fair imitation of Stan Laurel. 'Are these them – I mean, er – is this they?'

'I dunno,' intoned the sergeant, stroking his fiery ginger moustache with the back of one enormous, red hand. 'They reckon there was about 'alf-a-dozen on 'em, but – I dunno.' He thought for a while, which appeared to be a painful process. Then he said, 'Turn 'em out!' and tapped the desk with a forefinger the size of a banana.

We emptied our pockets. A rare collection came to light, some of it for the first time for months!

Five pathetic little personal pyramids were built under the unwavering, combined gazes of Frankenstein, the manager and the sergeant. Boiled sweets wrapped in fluff, fag cards, marbles, elastic bands, an engine name book, a month-old, mutilated copy of *Film Fun*, a school rubber, ball bearings in several sizes, a broken Dinky toy, safety pins, bits of string, one handkerchief in shades of grey (between five?) and two half-stubs of fourpenny tickets.

The only items of any value were the two penny packets of sweets which Vic produced.

[212]

'Where d'you get them?' The law pounced.

'Jus' now,' explained Vic. 'From the usherette. You can go an' ask 'er if you like.'

The manager picked up the evidence.

'Could be. We sell 'em.'

Frankenstein nodded.

''Ow long you been in the pictures?' the sergeant asked.

'All afternoon. Since before the firs' film started.'

I broke out in damp patches in case he asked me to describe the early part of the Deanna Durbin film when we had been otherwise engaged.

'I remember 'im comin' in, now I think about it,' Frankenstein put in – very fairly, I thought – pointing at Vic. 'Very early on it was.'

The sergeant had another think and came up with the direct approach. 'You ain't been in Woolworth's, 'ave you?'

We shook our heads.

'Not this afternoon?'

We shook them again.

'Stealin' stuff?'

More vigorous shakes.

'Right, then. Don't do it again!' he said illogically, but nobody argued. He put on his helmet and moved to the door. He opened it – but he had to get in a parting shot before he went.

'Seein' as 'ow it 'appens to be a 'A' picture, 'ow come you five got in unaccomp'nied? An' don't tell me you're midgets from Bertram Mills' Circus!'

Vic looked him straight in the eye and lied magnificently: 'We came with my Dad –' and before the law could nip in with the obvious question – ''e went 'ome early. 'E only came to see Deanna Durbin!'

'You're a little liar!' snapped the manager – pretty

viciously, I thought – as soon as the door closed. 'And another little thing – how come only two ticket stubs between five?'

'I lost mine,' said Albie.

'I chucked mine away,' said Spud.

'I ate mine,' said Georgie. 'I'm always eatin' things!'

'An' summat else,' bellowed Frankenstein, who appeared to have turned against us now the law had departed. 'They was sittin' in the shillin' seats!'

The manager pursed his lips – more like a magistrate than ever he looked.

'Unaccompanied juveniles – two fourpenny tickets – sitting in the best seats,' he mused – and gave Frankenstein a look which I recognised of old.

We were in the street in thirty seconds flat.

'Well, I like that!' said Vic. 'I don't mind gettin' chucked out of 'is crummy picture-house, but fancy that ole copper thinkin' we'd go round Woolie's pinchin' stuff. Like as though we was dishonest or summat!'

'I missed Bogart,' I said sadly.

'I 'spect it was the usual stuff,' said Albie, balance-walking along the wall of the Baptist Church. 'Gettin' in trouble with the Dead End Kids an' all that. Mus' be terrible bein' Dead End Kids. Always in trouble!'

His face was dead-pan as he concentrated on leaping over the church gate.

I saw the Bogart film on the telly the other night.

We didn't miss much.

No Way Back from Coventry

I once worked out how many hours of our schooldays were spent in the playground. Whatever the merits of the education on offer in the classrooms there was no disputing the infinite variety of lessons we learned on that congested asphalt yard and in the murky corners behind the bogs.

We did a great deal of fighting. Individuals, small groups and entire classes punched their way, happily or angrily according to the seriousness of the dispute, through successive morning and afternoon breaks. Easter was a popular season with the dedicated scrappers. Neither frostbite nor sun-stroke was likely to affect the combatants in the spring, and the quality and quantity of the punch-ups was a credit to our mothers and their fried bread breakfasts. Occasionally, a fight between two outstanding characters would bring all other hostilities to a temporary halt. There was such an event that Easter in '39.

I reckon the set-to between Harry Bidwell and Josher Unwin must have been the fiercest and best supported playground fight I ever saw. The whole school turned out to watch. Well, I mean, it isn't every day the Head Monitor gets involved in a scrap. Especially when he's a cheerful, matey sort of kid like Harry.

I never did know what sparked it off. When you were barely twelve the fourteen-year-olds in Standard VI were in a world apart. All I did know was that about ninety per cent of the spectators were on Harry's side.

'Go on, 'Arry, smarmalise 'im,' yelled my mate Albie.

'What started it off?' I enquired, between bouts of cheering. Always wanting to know the ins and outs of everything, as my Gramp would have said.

'I dunno,' Albie answered. 'It don't matter, does it? As long as Josher Unwin gets thumped.'

Josher ranked high among the dozen or so nasty pieces of work in the top school. Black hair, dark eyes, swarthy skin and dead crafty – some kids used to say he'd been left behind by the gipsies when they got moved off from behind the gas works some years back. He certainly lived a long way from the school compared with most of us, over the other side of the canal bridge.

'Watch 'is elbows, 'Arry!'

'Fight fair, Josher!'

'Go on, 'Arry, give 'im a Chinese upper-cut!'

The fight raged furiously for more than five minutes, the combatants driving each other back and forth across the confined space between the woodwork hut and the bogs. It was a lovely fight while it lasted – a real, barefist, playground classic. No prowling teacher in sight, so they slugged it out, toe to toe, knuckle to knuckle, bleeding nose versus split lip, a swelling eye for a bruised cheek.

And then it ended. Suddenly and unexpectedly.

One second Harry had Josher pinned up against the hut, pummelling his head with both fists, the next he was rolling on the asphalt clutching his lower abdomen.

''E kneed 'im in the bollocks!' howled Albie, leaping up and down on his legs and holding his own groin in a great show of sympathy and anger. 'Josher done 'im, the rotten bugger!'

There were howls of anguish from the ring-side as Harry rolled in what looked to us like mortal agony.

'Get 'im!' roared some of the big kids from the top class, Harry's pals. 'Don't let 'im get away!'

But he had already got away. Squirming, wriggling, dodging, feinting, Josher reached the gate and was off down the street at twenty to the dozen.

'Dirty coward!' we yelled after him. 'Jus' you wait till you comes to school nex' time.'

''E'll be back tomorrow,' said Albie. 'An' then 'e won't 'alf cop out.'

But he wasn't back tomorrow. He kept away for the better part of a week and then came creeping back with a doctor's note to say he'd had a chill.

'Get worse 'n a chill when 'Arry sets eyes on 'im,' muttered Albie.

We were both waiting eagerly in the playground when the bell went, making sure of a front ring-side view when hostilities recommenced.

But nothing happened. Standard VI came bounding and leaping down the stairs and into the yard and carried on playing marbles and tag and shooting-in and tripping up all us little kids as if it was a normal day.

'Crikey!' exploded Albie. 'Don't tell me 'Arry's gonna let 'im get away with it.'

My opinion of Harry, both as Head Monitor and gladiator, slipped several notches. He was just standing in the middle of the yard, chatting with a few of his cronies, as if last week had never happened.

Josher appeared at last. He cast his beady eyes around, like an animal scenting danger. Then, deciding there was none, he strolled over to join a gaggle of kids playing with fag-cards. As he arrived they collected their cards and moved off to the farthest corner by the bike shed. Josher made to join in with the footballers, but the nearest one picked up the ball and walked away with it. When he started climbing the lavatory wall, everyone playing in and around the bogs took to the fresh air.

'Blimey! Nobody's 'avin' nothin' to do with Josher,' I remarked unnecessarily.

'Course not,' said a big kid passing by. ''E bin sent to Coventry, ain't 'e!'

Albie gave me a blank sort of look, blanker than usual. 'Sent where?'

'Coventry,' I said, not quite as puzzled as Albie because I'd heard this saying somewhere before, though I couldn't quite place where or the exact meaning.

'No, 'e ain't,' said Albie. ''E's still 'ere.'

'It's one o' them things people say but don't mean,' I explained.

'What do people say 'em for, then, if they don't mean 'em? What's the sense in sayin' somebody's gone to Coventry when they're over there leanin' up against the wall?'

'Nobody said 'e'd ackchully *gone* to Coventry, they jus' said 'e'd been *sent* there,' I said feebly.

'Well, that's daft, ennit. I mean to say, if 'e've been sent, 'e've still gone jus' the same, but 'e ain't 'cos 'e's still over there like I said!'

Albie pointed out the figure of Josher, propping up the side of the school, as though he considered my sight must be failing.

'Albie, it's a kind of a motto or a proverb or somethin'! Grown-ups say things like that. My Gramp's always sayin' 'em. Like when you asks 'im where 'e's goin' an' 'e don't want nobody to know, 'e says, "To Jericho to see the bulls".'

'What bulls?'

'Oh never mind!'

'What's it got to do with goin' to Coventry?'

'Nothin', Albie, nothin' at all,' I said wearily. 'I was jus' tryin' to explain. What grown-ups says an' what they means is two diff'rent things! Bein' sent to Coventry means you don't 'ave nothin' to do with nobody.'

I often got things right given enough time.

'Nothin' at all?' enquired Albie, aghast.

'Nothin',' I declared with finality.

We watched fascinated for the remainder of the break as Standard VI busied themselves with having nothing to do with Josher Unwin. And in the succeeding days they polished the technique and enlarged their field of operations until Josher had no friend or ally in any part of the school.

'Like a leper, ain't 'e,' said Albie with a rare flash of historical-biblical-medical expertise. 'All by 'isself without nobody!'

It was some days later Albie and me were taking a short cut to school along Canal Row, where the original bargees' cottages overlooked the old canal, when we heard the insistent, high-pitched clanging of a warning bell.

'Fire engine,' beamed Albie.

I gave him my look of utter contempt.

'Don't be daft,' I said.

'Well, it ain't Sunday so it can't be Christ Church,' scoffed Albie, very ironic.

'It's the ambulance, ennit,' I informed him. 'I should've thought you could tell the diff'rence between a fire engine an' an ambulance by your age. Our kid could tell you that an' he's only eight.'

'That ain't never —' Albie began as the chocolate brown vehicle with the red crosses on its sides swung into Canal Row ahead of us. 'Blimey!' he concluded. 'They must've changed the bell!'

Ambulances fascinated me as much as fire engines and steam rollers. Almost as much as railway engines. Almost – but not quite. In a different sort of way. It was a weird, unhealthy attraction, depriving me of all power of escape until it either disappeared from view or stopped to load or unload its grisly burden before my incredulous eyes.

The headlamps on the shiny black mudguards hypnotised me like two shimmering, glass eyes. It was stopping. My God, it was going to stop right in front of me. A cackle of women with prams and shopping bags and nothing else to do gathered on the pavement. As the driver nipped round to open the rear door, they formed an inquisitive guard of honour from the gutter to the cottage door.

'C'mon,' urged Albie, tugging at the sleeve of my jersey, 'we'll be late.'

The driver and his mate were running the beady-eyed gauntlet, carrying the stretcher into the house. On it was a folded red blanket. No body. The thrill was yet to come.

''Urry up!' Albie was pleading now. 'You know what'll 'appen if we're late again. It'll be three on each 'and this time!'

Not even the fear of a hundred on each hand in front of the whole school could have shifted me at that instant. 'You go on, Albie, I'll catch you up.'

There was an awful hush in the street when the men had gone into the house. A wispy-haired woman in a pinny and floppy slippers came out of a house up the street and joined the huddle, spreading her bit of tittle-tattle around the gawping listeners.

'Blood ev'rywhere!' I heard her say and I shoved my

[220]

head between a pair of shopping baskets for fear of missing something. 'Awful, it was. Gawd knows 'ow long 'e'd bin there when our Arthur found 'im. Bleedin' like a pig, 'e was.'

My heart looped the loop. I was in for a more appalling nightmare than I had envisaged. I couldn't possibly leave now. Not even at the risk of two hundred on each hand.

The latch clicked like a pistol shot. An unseen hand opened the door. The uniformed driver came out backwards from the dingy, narrow passage, his hands showing up white against the wooden handles of the stretcher. The red blanket was bright in the cheerless, grey street. Did it look redder than when it went in? Now I could see the man at the other end of the stretcher, shuffling forward, trying not to fall over the brass door-step or knock his elbow on the stone lintel. And then I forced myself to look down at the face above the red blanket. The yellowy face on the white, white pillow. Unshaven for two or three days. Fifty years old? Or sixty? Or a hundred? It was only a glimpse but it would last me a lifetime. A yellow, sunken face that belonged to a man in limbo, hovering between living and dying. Strands of greying hair over the creased skin of his bald head. Thin lips, the same colour as the rest of his pallid face, drawn in tight against toothless gums.

But no blood anywhere. At least, none that I could see. From the colour of that pitiful face on the pillow, it could have all been drained out of him!

The driver slammed the door, folded up the rear step and climbed into his cab. The show was over. But its central character was left with me for life. Diminishing, certainly, as the years raced by, but still there today, tucked away in one of memory's small corners but clear and vivid when fetched out for inspection.

The bell rang when I was still a quarter of a mile short of the school gate. I got a haymaking thump round the ear that made my head sing a variety of songs when I eventually stumbled into the classroom, but I escaped the threatened three on each hand. The deafness in my left ear improved towards evening and I was able to eavesdrop on my Dad's supper-time conversation with my Mum. Tucked away behind *Film Fun*, I listened open-mouthed to the hushed exchanges.

'Suicide,' whispered Dad.

'Never,' gasped Mum, who was a non-church-going Christian and against suicide.

'Dead when they found 'im.'

I would have loved to chip in and query that positive statement but that would have been the end of that and there was much I still wanted to know.

'Cut 'is throat,' said Dad.

Film Fun twitched uncontrollably.

'Never,' said Mum, and couldn't resist adding: 'what with?'

'Razor.'

'Good God!' exclaimed Mum, not altogether religiously.

There were a lot of medical questions I wanted to ask but I stifled them.

Later on, Old Mr Pinnock from the end house came in.

'I knew 'im, Will Packer it were,' he said for openers and we all knew who he meant. 'Worked down the running shed.'

'Wasn't always a railwayman, was 'e?' 'E was a cleaner.' asked Dad.

'No. Afore that 'e used to be a clerk over the tobacco factory.'

'What the 'eck is a clerk doin' down the running shed?'

Mr Pinnock licked his lips. There was much to tell. I

[222]

snuggled down even more self-effacingly behind the pages of my comic.

'You must remember. Some of the clerks in the tobacco offices worked on in the General Strike. Used to dodge the pickets an' climb over the wall. When the lads went back they sent the lot of 'em to Coventry. Most of 'em left after a bit, but Will stuck it for six years. Then he had a breakdown. Didn't work for a twelve-month. Then his brother got him a job inside. That was all he could get him – cleaning engines down the running shed.'

There was a lengthy silence before my Mum put the question that was occupying my mind, too. 'That's not why 'e done it, is it? You know, committed suicide. Not because of what happened to him all them years ago?'

'You never can tell, can you?' mused Mr Pinnock. 'Different things affects different people different ways. One thing I do know. He weren't never the same bloke again after his breakdown. An' seeing the breakdown was caused by six years of being sent to Coventry by a whole factory full o' people – well, it do make you wonder, don't it?'

'It do indeed,' murmured Dad and then added brightly, 'I s'pose he got on all right with the blokes down the shed?'

Mr Pinnock pursed his lips and shook his head, slowly, many times, delaying the words that would complete the sad little story. 'Never spoke to no one,' he said at last. 'Got so used to not speaking to nobody over the 'baccy factory he never spoke to nobody down the shed neither.'

'No one?'

'Not to my knowledge. Far as I know he never spoke to a living soul these last ten years.'

I lay in bed, wide awake into the eeriest depths of the night, with a face close to my own on the pillow. Sunken, yellow cheeks – wispy, grey hair – blank, unseeing eyes. The dead face of Will Packer, strike-breaker and suicide.

The next morning Josher Unwin wasn't at school.

I stuck it until the end of morning break and then I went and knocked on the door of Josher's classroom.

'Please, Mr Ratcliffe, do you know where Unwin is, sir?'

'I do not,' snapped Thumper Ratcliffe, the scourge of Standard VI. 'And if you do, I'd be glad to relieve you of the information.'

'What I mean is, sir, can I 'ave permission to go round 'is 'ouse?'

'What for?'

'To see 'e's all right, Mr Ratcliffe. Just in case –'

'He'd better not be all right,' thundered Thumper. 'If he's all right he ought to be here. He'd better be very far from all right.'

'But 'e might 'ave –'

'Might have what?' cut in Thumper. 'What are you blathering about? Whose class are you in, anyway? Stop wasting my time.'

He slammed the door in my face. I strode purposefully along the corridor towards my own classroom, walked straight past it, through the lobby, across the playground and into the street. And then began to run. Hell for leather down King Street, into Queen Street, across Princes Street, down the backs behind the shirt factory, past the Co-op bakery, under the first railway bridge and on to the canal tow-path. Then down to a gasping jog-trot as I turned over the hump-backed bridge and headed towards the single row of tiny, terraced houses that backed on to the canal on its further side.

Josher was clearly visible playing in his back-yard.

An indescribable surge of relief swept over me. 'Josher!' I yelled.

He looked up and ran indoors. He probably didn't recognise me, anyway. He was in the top school and I was two light years away from such exalted status, so he could hardly be expected to recognise such small fry.

Still, my mission was accomplished. Josher was alive and well and not looking particularly suicidal.

'Josher!' I hollered once more, still obsessed by a desire to tell him not to treat being sent to Coventry as if it was the end of the world.

Josher's mother came waddling out of the house hoisting her sleeves and flexing her biceps. It must have been his mother because it was the same black hair, swarthy skin, crafty eyes, only it was female and a good few years older.

'Gerroff!' she screeched, waving a very solid-looking fist in the air. 'You just bugger off and leave our Cedric alone.'

Cedric! Well swipe me!

'But, Mrs Unwin, I only –'

'You deaf or summat? Clear off. You couldn't speak to him at school so why come round pestering him at home? Spoiling his last few days.'

His last few days! Good God, does she know what he's going to do? Do suicides discuss it first? With their mothers? I'd never discuss it with mine – I'd have to make my mind up fast and get on with it.

'Mrs Unwin!' I tried once more.

'Will you sod off or d'you want the dog set on you?' she queried, opening the back gate. 'Just gerroff back your own side of the bridge and leave the lad in peace.'

R.I.P Josher. Now what was I going to do? Back to school and another clump round the ear for leaving the building without permission? Or round to Old Town police station? (*Please sergeant, I wish to report a potential suicide. Thank you very much, sonny. Now you just run along home to your mother.*)

I found it even more difficult to get off to sleep that night. I not only shared my pillow with Will, but with Josher, too.

He wasn't at school the next day. Nor the rest of the week. But neither was there anything in the evening paper or on the wireless, and no chatter on the playground grapevine or late-night visitations from Mr Pinnock.

On Saturday morning, after I'd finished my weekly stint of errands, I made my way along the canal and over the hump-backed bridge. The house was deserted. The uncurtained kitchen window proclaimed its emptiness for all to see. The big cast-iron mangle was gone from outside the scullery door and the little shed made from GWR wood and asbestos sheets had also disappeared. I went round the front and all the windows were white-washed. Not only Josher but the entire Unwin household had decamped.

'They been chucked out,' Albie informed me later in the day as we sat on our coal-bunk flicking shiny slivers of best Welsh steam coal at Mrs Collins' washing.

'What for?' I stopped in mid-flick.

'They ain't paid their rent,' said Albie smugly. 'They been moved over Ashurst.'

The Ashurst council estate was in the crummiest part of the town. The rows of little flat-fronted, contiguous houses were filled to overflowing with families who were dumped there when they couldn't – or wouldn't – pay their rent.

'Cheap an' nasty,' I once heard my Mum say. 'They'll have to carry me out of this house feet first before they'll get me over there!'

I couldn't see it was really that bad because I'm sure

from some of the bedroom windows they must have had an uninterrupted view of the main London to Bristol line. I could lie in bed and HEAR the trains where I lived but – well, I mean, just fancy being able to sit up in bed and actually SEE them!

'I s'pose we won't be seein' 'im at our school no more,' I opined as I scored a direct hit on a pillow case.

'Course not,' said Albie scathingly. 'They got their own school, ain't they. Ashurst Elementary.'

It must have been two years later Josher Unwin made the headlines in our local rag: BODY OF YOUTH FOUND ON LINE.

'How did it happen, Dad?'

'You can read, can't you?' said Dad. 'You know as much as I do.'

'But I don't see why he was crossing the tracks at night, in the black-out.'

'Fooling around as like as not. Typical of his sort. See where he come from?' Dad tapped the paper with his finger. 'Ashurst estate. They're all bloody stupid over Ashurst.'

'It was an accident, wasn't it, Dad?'

'Course it was an accident. You don't think the stupid little beggar did it on purpose, do you?'

Did I? I don't know. Not to this day I don't know for sure.

All I do know is that it must be a devil of a long road back from Coventry.

Christmas 1980

It was bitterly cold.

The fluttering snow flakes disappeared as if by magic as they touched down gently on the asphalt driveway but on the grass and flower beds they were beginning to settle.

My wife tugged at the sleeve of my new sheepskin car coat.

'Let's go inside,' she whispered.

The little chapel seemed to be about one degree warmer than the world outside but at least it locked out the east wind.

We sat about half-way down. I wondered how many rows of family and new friends there would be. I looked round the half-dozen faces already gathered, but there were none from our past. There were just two men; one was ten years too young, the other more like twenty years too old.

There were flowers everywhere. On the altar, on the steps, on the window ledges. Sheaves of yellow and white chrysanthemums, sprays of red carnations, sprigs of holly, two huge vases of magnificent white-spathed arum lilies. How I loathe arum lilies!

My wife was on her knees. I wondered what she was

saying. It couldn't be anything personal because she had never known him. Probably a few kind thoughts for all the others who had gone on ahead, including my Mum and Dad whom she loved almost as much as I did. She had a great capacity for loving all those who were dear to me. I wished she could have known this particular one. But she could have only known him as a boy because I only knew him as a boy. Our ways parted very early, a long time ago, getting on for forty years ago, long before she arrived in my life.

A few more strangers tip-toed in. They sat behind us. I wanted to turn round and see if – but they wouldn't be, of course. It was too far away from where it had all happened. More than a hundred miles. A hundred miles and forty years on. I told myself for the umpteenth time that there would not be anyone else present whom I could possibly know. I wouldn't have been here myself but for the million to one chance of meeting this bloke in The Steam Train.

I heard the faint slamming of car doors in the street outside and I could visualise the tiny procession forming up at the porch. By the time you get into your fifties you're getting quite familiar with the ritual. A sudden blast of cold air on the back of the neck, a feeling of imminent action, a tightness across one's chest like the climactic moment on the big dipper. Will it come now – or now – or now – oh! for God's sake get started, man, we all know the form.

I am the resurrection and the life saith the Lord; he that believeth in me, though he were dead, yet shall he live.

Did he believe in Him?

How should I know? I remember going on a Sunday school treat with him once. But even that was a fiddle. I fixed it for him. He never even put in an appearance at Sunday school.

[229]

We brought nothing into this world and it is certain we can carry nothing out.

Well, the first part of that was certainly true. He had nothing when I knew him. We had totally nothing when we started out. I wondered if he had accumulated much in the intervening years. Not that it would make any odds now. He was taking nothing out.

The droning voice drew abreast and passed on with a swift swish of white surplice and black cassock. Then *he* passed me, jogging gently on the shoulders of four nondescript figures in black overcoats who had never even known him. I would have liked to have carried him. It didn't look as though he had grown very much since we used to sit on our coal-bunk and chuck coal at Mrs Collins' washing. A single spray of flowers seemed to cover the top of the coffin.

I counted the shuffling figures who followed behind. Four couples and an old man on his own. None that I knew. The small, greying woman would be his widow. But if the young man on whom she leaned was their son, then he took after his mother's family. Too tall, too heavily built, wrong colouring. I couldn't see anyone who resembled him at all.

We sang the twenty-third psalm. At least, the vicar, the funeral director, the four bearers and my wife sang. The rest stared at their books and were afraid to risk it in such a small company. I found myself hypnotised by the coffin, remembering all the other coffins I had seen on their way over the years, recalling quite unexpectedly a night when I followed an unknown coffin through the candle-lit streets to the catholic church.

'We are gathered here today,' began the vicar who had suddenly appeared in the pulpit, 'to give thanks for the life of our departed brother Albert Edward. I regret to say I did not know him in life –'

But I did, I wanted to cry out. Let me get up there and I'll tell you some tales about Albert Edward. I'll tell you about the golden days, the beautiful years when we were young and didn't know it, adventures with runaway horses up the crossing, getting into the pictures and football matches without paying, digging up his Dad's back garden and finding hidden treasure.

'I know that his loving presence will be sadly missed by his devoted wife and son –'

And by me! Maybe not so much, not so often, but he is a part of my life, too. I'd like to stake my claim to the thirties, especially that last, tranquil year before the war. Our year. Nineteen thirty-eight.

'Let us pray.'

I found it difficult. Albie wasn't the sort of person you could pray for very easily. I got the feeling he would be embarrassed and start giggling or thumping me in the chest if he heard me praying for him. So I thought about him instead. About his skinny little matchstick arms and the holes in his shoes and the faith he had that I would always be able to get him out of things or into places. About the troubles we had halved by sharing and the simple pleasures we had enjoyed by the same token.

And then the thought that I had been pushing aside for ages came bursting through. Why did we never meet again when we were grown men? Why did neither of us make the effort? Or any of the others in that gang, come to that?

I always thought we would some day. But not now. Not in this world. Fifty-four was no age to be dead. We might have met again when we were very old and sat on a park bench and smoked our pipes and dreamed of Castles and Kings, the Cheltenham Flyer and the up-milk from Fishguard, Trip Day and all the fun of the fair.

Only fifty-four. Yet he had enjoyed thirty odd years

more life than Vic and a lot more kids down our street who started the war in short trousers and ended it six feet under foreign soil or a thousand feet below some rolling ocean.

So maybe at fifty-four I was already enjoying an extension. Living on time borrowed from Vic's lost generation. I remembered my Uncle George.

'And now, let us join together in singing his favourite hymn, "Praise, my soul, the King of Heaven".'

Albie's favourite hymn! I didn't think he knew any hymns. How forty years can change a man. Perhaps his wife was religious. They obviously were not church-going people – the vicar said he didn't know him. And then it came to me. Morning assembly at school. We only had about twenty hymns in our repertoire and we knew them all by heart. This was one of them. I put down the hymn book. I did not need it. I sang with gusto.

Soon after that, they picked up Albie for very nearly the last time and bore him back down the aisle to where the gleaming limousine would be waiting for the final trek to the cemetery. I had no idea where the local cemetery was and I had no desire to find out. I am not exactly addicted to the grave-side ritual. I felt that I could trust that bit to his family. I was glad I had come, but enough was enough.

The people remaining in the chapel were saying a last prayer. My wife was on her knees again. I leaned forward and rested my eyelids on my thumb and forefinger and thought some more. About how the war had come and Albie's Dad had been one of the first down our street to be called up and had survived Dunkirk only to go and get killed in an accident in a tank in Egypt. And how, almost before I'd had time to

[232]

ask him what sort of tank it was, Albie had been whipped off to his Gran at Gillingham, never to return.

'Come on, love. I know how you feel,' whispered my wife, giving me the customary tug on the sleeve. 'Everybody's gone.'

I rushed out of the church because I wanted to see what the hearse was like. It was very flash. Low and sleek and not a bit like old Charlie's pride and joy that he used to polish so lovingly in the street outside J. J. Jones and Sons (Undertakers). Albie would have appreciated old Charlie driving him on his last lap in that gleaming, square-sided, glass box with a Rolls-Royce engine. Ah, well, you can't have everything – not in death any more than in life!

'Hello, me old mate. It is you, isn't it? Long, long time no see, eh?'

I recognised him instantly.

'Georgie.' I swallowed once or twice as he felt for my hand and gripped it in his own. 'It certainly is a hell of a long time.'

I thumped him on the shoulder half-a-dozen times while we weighed each other up and wondered what else there was to say.

'Aren't you going to introduce me?'

'Of course. I'm sorry. Georgie, this is my wife. And this is Georgie. He was one of us, you know, one of our gang.'

Georgie shook hands with my wife and said: 'We had some fair old times when we were kids. My God, didn't we, though. When I think of the things we got up to –!'

'D'you live round this way?' I asked him.

'About fifteen miles away, that's all. Same local paper, that's how I knew. I ran into him once, about seven or eight years ago, in Marks and Sparks. He said he wouldn't have recognised me.'

'I did. Right away. No mistaking that nose!'

Georgie grinned.

'He remembered you all right. We talked a lot about you.'

'I should bloody well hope so,' I said. 'He was my best mate.'

'You still living in the old metropolis?' Georgie asked.

'Still there. On the new estate where the Manor House used to be. You know the old street's gone, I suppose?'

'Yes. I was passing through a few years back. I stopped off to have a quiet reminisce. There was nothing left to latch on to. Far as I could see there's a Tesco where the old canal used to be. Anyway, how did you come to hear about – Albie?'

'You'd never believe it,' I began. 'I was in The Steam Train – you wouldn't know it – only yesterday lunchtime. There was this chap there, rep. for some electronics firm or something, I'd met him a few times, often talked about how big his area was, stretching right over here. Must have mentioned Albie some time or other. He was looking for me – had the local paper there, must have been the same one you saw it in. Recognised the surname, being so uncommon – brought the paper in case he saw me – and here I am.'

'Let's move, shall we? This wind is cutting me in half,' my wife said, shivering.

We bent our heads into the gale and moved into the street.

'How's about a drink, then?' I suggested brightly, checking my watch. 'We've got time.'

'I haven't,' Georgie replied. ''Fraid I've got an important appointment first thing this afternoon. I'll have to dash.'

'You've got a good job, I suppose?' I recalled Georgie's university education.

'Not bad.' He reached inside his coat and came out with a small, white, printed card. 'Give us a ring any time you're down this way again. Come and have a meal with us.'

He took out his car keys and unlocked the door of a green Ford Granada.

'Sorry it's been such a rush.' He shrugged and turned to my wife to shake hands. 'Nice to meet you. Do look us up when you can. Love you to meet the family.'

He slid into the car and switched on.

I tapped on the window.

'What happened to Spud?' I asked.

'Don't know,' he replied, winding down the glass. 'Went in the RAF, didn't he? Well, cheers for now, me old mate. Hope to see you in happier circs. next time, eh?'

We shook hands through the window and he started to move off.

'Georgie!' I yelled. 'Remember Vic? He was missing, presumed drowned, just a month before it ended. He put his age on so he could –'

The Granada leaped into a vacancy in the traffic flow. It was a V registration.

'Quite a nice chap,' my wife said without enthusiasm.

'But there was so much to say.' I stood on the kerb, mildly stunned, vaguely upset. 'So much to tell him and so many questions to ask. I mean – well, I don't even know what he died of, do I? I mean, only fifty-four, same age as me. I don't feel as if I've got a foot anywhere near the grave yet? I wonder –'

'Does it matter?' she said as we moved away. 'Does it really matter?'

'Not really, I suppose,' I said after a pause.

[235]

'I don't think this chap we've just met was close like you and Albie were.'

I rushed to agree. 'Good God, no. Me and Albie, we were special. The others – well, they were all part of the gang – all lived down the street – couldn't help growing up together – but Albie and me –'

I guided her towards the lounge bar of The White Swan. We sat in a corner and it was lovely and warm. I undid my car coat which was an early Christmas present.

'It looks smart,' said the donor. 'What are you giving me for Christmas?'

'I'll think of something,' I teased.

And I suddenly remembered Christmas 1938. The last Christmas before the war. 'D'you know what I had for Christmas nineteen thirty-eight?' I asked rhetorically.

'Surprise me,' she said.

'I had my first decent clockwork train set. Eight sections of rail, a tank engine and six coal trucks. I overwound the engine on Boxing Day and bust the spring and had to push it up and down the track for the rest of the year.'

I sipped my pint of best bitter.

'I just thought of something else, too.'

'Don't tell me you remember what Albie had for Christmas forty years ago,' she sighed.

'As a matter of fact, I do. I went over his house straight after breakfast, as soon as I'd had a few goes with my train set. He had this meccano spread all over the kitchen floor.'

'You're incredible.' She sipped her peach brandy and shook her head disbelievingly. 'You and Albie. You and that gang of kids. You seem to recall those days as though they were only last year. I reckon you could write a book about it all.'

[236]

I looked her straight in the eye over the rim of my glass.

'I reckon I could,' I said. 'I damn well reckon I could.'